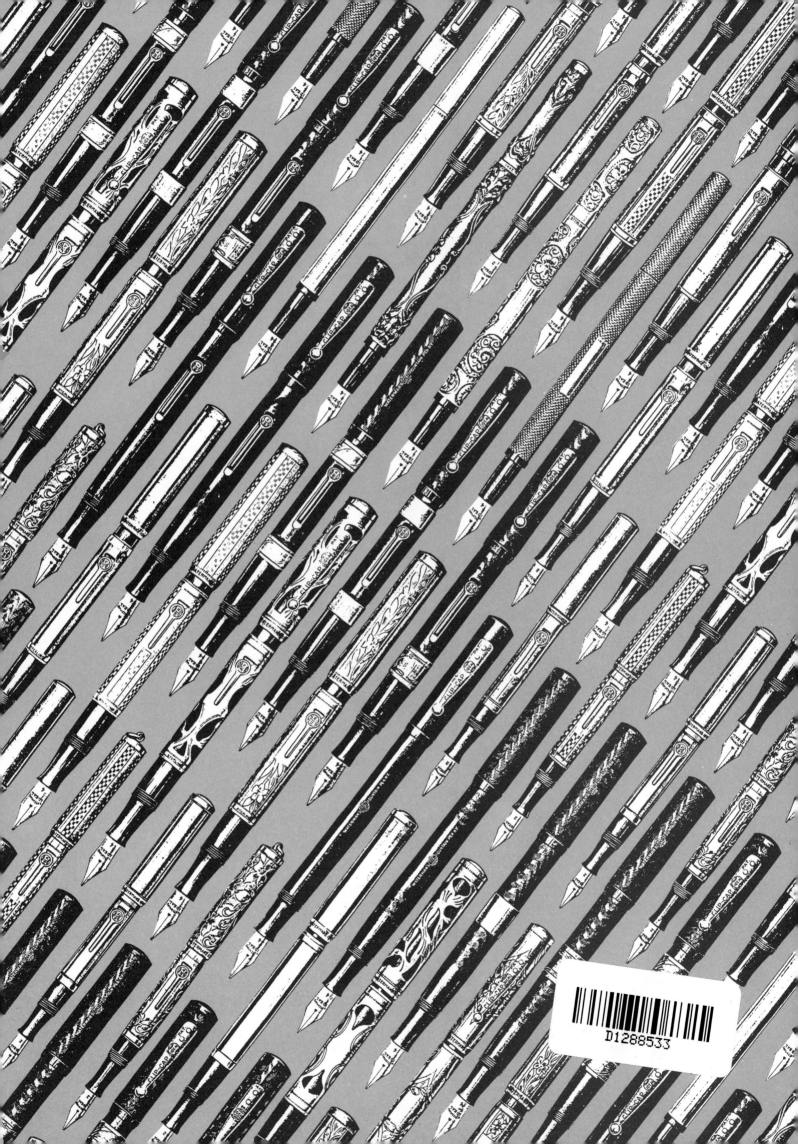

FOUNTAIN
PENS

FOUNTAIN PENS

THE COLLECTOR'S GUIDE TO SELECTING, BUYING, AND ENJOYING NEW AND VINTAGE FOUNTAIN PENS

Jonathan Steinberg

COURAGE BOOKS

AN IMPRINT OF
RUNNING PRESS
PHILADELPHIA, PENNSYLVANIA

Canadian Representatives:
General Publishing Co., Ltd.
30 Lesmill Road, Don Mills
Ontario M3B 2T6

9 8 7 6 5 4 3 2 1
Digit on the right indicates the number of this printing

Library of Congress
Cataloging-in-Publication Number
93-85548

ISBN 1-56138-221-3

This book was designed and produced by
Quintet Publishing Limited
6 Blundell Street
London N7 9BH

Senior Editor: Laura Sandelson
Creative Director: Richard Dewing
Designer: Ian Hunt
Editor: Lydia Darbyshire
Photographer: Chas Wilder

Typeset in Great Britain by
Central Southern Typesetters, Eastbourne
Manufactured in Singapore by
Bright Arts Pte. Limited
Printed in Hong Kong by
Leefung-Asco Printers Limited

ACKNOWLEDGEMENTS

The author wishes to acknowledge the efforts of, and
thank the following people who gave their invaluable
assistance (as well as their pens) in the writing of this
work: Peter Miller, Edward Fingerman, Brad Nelson
Torelli, Mario Frigerio, Peter Liebowitz, Jerry Jirard,
Dr. James King, Raffaella Simoni Malaguti and
Gianluca Malaguti, Geoffrey Berliner, Piero
Premoselli Giusseppi Brunori, and to Pier Gustafson
for the handwriting samples on page 7.

Published by Courage Books
an imprint of Running Press Book Publishers
125 South Twenty-Second Street
Philadelphia, Pennsylvania 19103-4299

CONTENTS

INTRODUCTION

W hy is it that when fountain pens are mentioned today most people think either of a large, rounded black pen with a huge, two-tone nib that dealers recommend be thrown away when it goes wrong, or of the piece of tin-nibbed plastic they may have used at school when they last had to write anything substantial?

The revival of interest in old fountain pens has been partly spurred by disenchantment with the pens currently available. The chief executive who uses a cheap, throwaway ballpoint pen is making a strong statement about his personal style; no chairman of a major international company is going to sign interoffice memos with a colored crayon.

Not only are the look of the pen and the writing different; writing with a vintage fountain pen *feels* different. The reason for the difference lies in the method of construction of the nib. Even a cursory glance will show that using a ballpoint pen offers no opportunity to impart character to handwriting. Modern pens that have a stub or a chisel-point nib can be used to create something of the effect achieved by a vintage pen. On down strokes, for example, such a nib will describe broad lines because the surface presented by the nib to the paper will be broad; on cross strokes the lines will be thin because the surface presented will be thin. However, the relative inflexibility of the nib will mean that there will be little variation between the thick and thin lines.

The nibs made before World War II had the flexibility to describe a variety of lines. The nibs moved smoothly across the page, requiring no special effort on the part of the writer to think about the strokes being made. Only one company today, Omas, makes pens with flexible nibs, and it is the nib that makes the difference in writing style.

LEFT **Montblanc no. 12. This safety pen has a curled snake-type clip, which was common on mid-European pens of the 1920s.**

RIGHT **Handwriting samples made with a ballpoint pen; a modern fountain pen with a rigid nib and heavy ink flow; and an early fountain pen with a very flexible nib.**

Between its invention in the 1880s and its fall from general use in the face of the economic pressures created by the arrival of the cheap and ubiquitous ballpoint pen in the 1950s and 1960s, the fountain pen has a fascinating history. Manufacturers, especially between 1900 and 1935, went to great lengths to produce beautiful as well as functional models. Today, these pens are being collected all over the world, not only as elegant and attractive objects in themselves, but as pens to be used to impart style and character to what is written.

ABOVE & RIGHT **The differences between old flexible nibs and new rigid nibs. On the flexible nib the length between the air hole and the tip is long; on the new one that part of the nib is relatively** **short and stubby. In addition, the flexible nib has metal that is thinner just behind the iridium tip, whereas the modern one is of uniform thickness.**

The blaze in my neighbour's hayrick warms the tea in my samovar.

The blaze in my neighbour's hayrick warms the tea in my samovar

The blaze in my neighbour's hayrick warms the tea in my samovar.

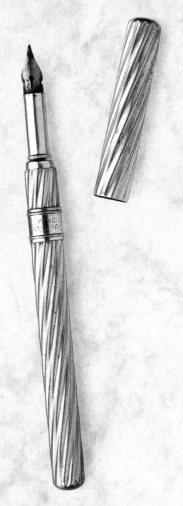

Ever since ancient scribes first put nib to papyrus, writing had been a laborious business, involving as it did the dipping of a quill in ink so that a few words could be written before the quill had to be dipped in ink again. The quill was a feather-shaft, specially cut to hold a small amount of ink. The point, produced by a quill cutter, wore out quickly, and after only a few days a new quill had to be cut. The introduction of longer-lasting metal nibs was welcomed, and the necessary flexibility could be ensured by the use of gold or, in less expensive pens, of steel. Even these had to be replaced after a relatively short time, but during the late 1820s a way was found of attaching a point to the tip of nib so that while the gold retained its flexibility it did not wear out quickly in heavy or extended use. Such tips were made of an extremely hard material – initially ruby and later the element iridium.

THE EARLY HISTORY OF THE FOUNTAIN PEN

CHAPTER I

LEFT **An exceptionally rare Eagle.**

ABOVE **Dipping pen set in 18-carat gold by S. Mordan & Co. Mordan was by far the most famous of the companies making dipping pens and propelling pencils, and claimed to dominate the pencil market throughout the 19th century. The early metal replacements for the quill, which did not contain an ink reservoir, had been known as penners. This non-hallmarked example, which dates from the mid-19th century, may have been made at Mordan's French workshops at 19 rue des Pyramides, Paris.**

A PEN WITHOUT END

The following extract is taken from the 1723 English translation of Monsieur M. Bion's work on Mathematical Instruments. This is his description and accompanying drawing of the fountain pen or "Plume sans fin" (a pen without end) as he called it:

"Of the Fountain Pen.– This instrument is composed of different pieces of brass, silver, &c.; and when the pieces F, G, H, are put together, they are about five inches long, and its diameter is about three lines. The middle piece, F, carries the pen, which ought to be well slit, and cut, and screwed into the inside of a little pipe, which is soldered to another pipe of the same bigness, as the lid, G; in which lid is soldered a male screw, for screwing on the cover: as likewise for stopping a little hole at the place I, and so hindering the ink from running through it. At the other end of the piece, F, there is a little pipe, on the outside of which the top-cover, H, may be screwed on. In this top-cover there goes a porte-craion, that is to screw into the last-mentioned little pipe, and so stop the end of the pipe at which the ink is poured in, by means of a funnel. When the aforementioned pen is to be used, the cover, G, must be taken off, and the pen a little shaken, in order to make the ink run freely. Note.– If the porte-craion does not stop the mouth of the piece, F, the air, by its pressure, will cause the ink to run out at once. Note, also, that some of these pens have seals soldered at their ends." (Taken from *Journal of the Society of Arts*, Vol. LIII, No. 2, 763.)

FIG. 114.

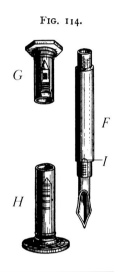

The real problem for most people was still the fact that the nib had to be dipped into ink every few characters. Quills used more ink as they wore out and the points became broader, and even though metal nibs used less ink and produced consistently finer lines, scribes still longed for a means of writing whereby the nib was not dipped continuously. Myths arose about pens that had their own ink supplies that could write for longer. One such fable current in the mid-17th century told how a king of Sweden, tiring of having to dip his quill into ink so often, had commissioned a pen that carried its own ink supply in its barrel. There is no evidence, however, that such a pen ever existed.

Rudimentary devices were used to capture more ink on the nib, but these did not function well because there was no method of metering the flow of ink onto the paper. It may have seemed that increasing the ink-holding capacity of a pen would automatically lead to a greater writing capacity, but that does not happen. If you merely fill a long, thin reservoir with ink and stick a "nib" at the bottom, ink will not flow smoothly – and it may not even flow at all. This fact was not apparent to all those who had been studying quills for centuries and who perceived the need to be for nothing more than a point with a reservoir behind it. It seemed to such people that it should be perfectly possible to produce a pen with an artificial reservoir simply by adapting what nature had already designed and what the world was already using. The truth was, of course, that quills had not been designed for writing, but for flying. There is no case on record of long-feathered birds ever having been able to write.

LEFT **A system used on some dipping pen nibs to capture ink on the underside of the nib.**

1819, and this example was made in 1825. Usually in the Penographic ink was made to flow to the nib by pulling back a valve behind the section. On this model, however, the ink flows continuously, and is prevented from flowing out

ABOVE & RIGHT **Scheffer's Penographic; 4⅝ inches. The Penographic was patented in**

when the pen is filled by putting on the cap, which inserts a pin into the channel in the feed under the nib. The pen is filled by removing the plug at the rear of the barrel and using an eyedropper to fill the pig's bladder inside with ink.

EARLY RESERVOIR SYSTEMS

Since the early years of the 18th century, craftsmen had been trying to produce pens that did not need dipping. Unfortunately, they did not understand that when ink comes out of the barrel and flows down the nib to the paper, it will tend to create a vacuum inside the barrel. After the initial flow of whatever ink is lying on the nib or quill, no further ink will flow to the paper, and attempts to force more ink from the reservoir to the nib will generally result in a blob of ink appearing on the paper.

The pens produced at this time did not work properly because they had no means of metering the flow of ink to the paper. Nevertheless, the craftsmen, mostly working in silver, concentrated on making the pens as beautiful as possible – even though they did not function as they were intended. Many of these pens were, inevitably, thrown away by their frustrated users, and few have survived. In consequence, when they are found today their value is enormous, although many, whose quills have disintegrated or fallen out, are scarcely recognizable as pens.

As the 19th century wore on, the ingenuity of the craftsmen in following this mistaken principle knew no bounds. Fine cotton was used to try to get a flow of ink, and the problem of ink leaking out of the silver vessel

all over the paper was corrected by using a pig's bladder or something similar to contain the ink. Rudimentary, but unsuccessful, attempts at metering the ink using balsa wood slats to hold the bladder open were also made.

In 1819 John Scheffer took out a patent for a "Penographic or Writing Instrument," in which the ink was caused to flow to the nib by exerting pressure on a lever and knob. Scheffer's pen consisted of an external metal case, with a cork stopper at the top and a cock tube near the bottom. Inside the case was an elastic tube formed of part of a goose quill and the pig's bladder. The lever acted on a valve or plug passing through the cock tube.

One of the most famous early fountain pens was patented by John Jacob Parker in 1832. (There is, in fact, no connection between that Parker and the pen manufacturer of the same name, although John Jacob Parker has been traced to Northampton in Britain, the town from which came the Parker family that settled in Janesville, Wisconsin, and founded the eponymous fountain pen company some 50 years later.) The 1832 patent was "for certain improvements in fountain pens," and Parker described his pen as having "a piston and rod in the barrel with which ink could be forced to the nib, to which it was delivered through a small, bell-mouthed tube, as required." The barrel,

PARKER'S 1832 PATENT

"John Jacob Parker obtained a patent (6288) in 1832, 'for certain improvements in fountain pens,' and he describes his pen (shown in Fig. 3) as having a piston, P, and rod in the barrel, B, with which to force ink to the nib as required, to which it is delivered through a small bell-mouthed tube, T. To fill the barrel, he says, dip the end of the penholder into ink, and raise the piston by turning the outer case. In this specification we have the first mention of a so-called self-filling pen." A wire, W, attached to the inside of the cap, K, enters the ink-delivering passage, and prevents the outflow of ink when the cap is placed over the nib." (Taken from *Journal of the Society of Arts*, Vol. LIII, No. 2, 763.)

FIG. 3.

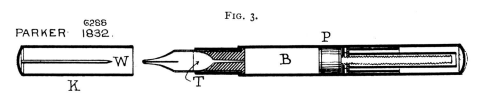

PARKER 6288 1832. W K T B P

according to Parker, was filled by dipping the end of the penholder in ink and raising the piston by turning the outer case, which is the first mention of a self-filling pen.

These early pens were, therefore, similar in concept to, if different in design from, the 20th-century pens that used either rubber sacks or pistons in properly sealed barrels. Other early 19th-century devices were designed to force the flow. Some had a button on the side by which pressure could be exerted on the pig's bladder, which made the process of writing a relatively fatiguing one; others employed a rudimentary feeding system, which sent some ink to the nib on down strokes, thereby solving a quarter of the problem, which was, presumably, better than no solution at all.

The next problem to be solved was to prevent ink flooding onto the paper. This challenge was met by inserting a sponge between the nib and the pig's bladder, which was filled by pressing a button.

A few faintly workable fountain pens were made in the early days in this way. Thomas Jefferson (1743–1826) certainly used a writing instrument that presumably satisfied his needs in not having to be dipped into ink every few characters. However, no patents were taken out for that implement, and not much is known of how it worked beyond the fact that it apparently used a rubber tube to connect the pen to an ink supply that was held higher than the paper. Although it probably did not have a proper device to feed ink to the paper, it is noteworthy that Jefferson's manuscripts are not characterized by ink blots. Either the pen worked or, alternatively, he did not use it much for formal writing.

RIGHT **1850s nickel and pig's bladder pen; manufacturer unknown. There were reservoir pens before the 1880s, but they did not work, were difficult to use, and now, in default of a nib, they are** seldom even recognized as pens. This example has a hole in the side of the barrel through which a finger is inserted to press the pig's bladder sack and so feed a blob of ink onto the nib. This should have made it unnecessary to keep on dipping the nib into the ink every few words as with a dipping pen. The pen may not have written properly and continuously, but one supposes that it was some kind of advance over the dipping pen itself.

The Channeled Feed

The major advance in fountain pen technology occurred when it was found that if air could flow up a channel and into the ink reservoir in properly measured amounts, a vacuum would not form and the ink would flow smoothly out of the reservoir.

The commercial fountain pen was probably invented in the 1880s by several different people. Early patents for working systems based on the same basic principle were recorded by the American company Paul E. Wirt and Americans Mabie, Todd & Bard, two companies producing dipping pens, and which no doubt saw the development as nothing more than a natural extension of their main business and therefore nothing to get too excited about. Also at this time – the early 1880s – Lewis E. Waterman, an insurance salesman, developed a workable fountain pen when he lost money by accidentally spilling ink over a contract that a wealthy client was on the point of signing. Realizing the potential of the pen as a revolutionary way of writing without having to dip the nib into ink every few words, Waterman took out a patent and set about telling the whole world about his invention.

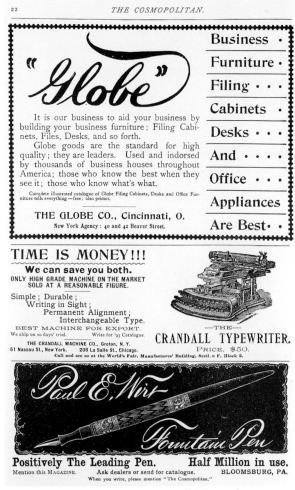

ABOVE An 1890s advertisement for Paul E. Wirt products.

L. E. Waterman's 1884 Patent

"Fig. 19 shows the feed bar of L. E. Waterman, in 1884 (3125). The ink reservoir, A, carries a point section, B, at one end, and the feed piece, C, fits tightly into the point section. An ink duct, D, is formed along the feed, and consists of longitudinal fissures or saw cuts. The nib, P, is secured between the feed and the point section, and ink is fed to the nib by gravity and capillarity, air being drawn into the reservoir along the fissures of the ink duct. Below are transverse sections of the feed bar showing two arrangements of ducts. It will be seen that the main groove contains in one case two minor grooves, and in the other three, very fine saw cut grooves. These commence at the back end, and extend nearly to the point as shown in the longitudinal section." (Taken from *Journal of the Society of Arts*, Vol. LIII, No. 2, 763.)

FIG. 19.

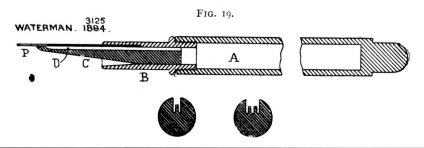

WATERMAN. 1884. 3125.

The new system depended on a feed with a channel in it being placed under the nib. Air would pass up the channel into the reservoir, while at the same time ink would flow, in the opposite direction but in equivalent amounts, through the feed onto the paper.

The channeled feed was basically a very simple device, and it was widely copied. The companies producing pens had to make their names in the market by emphasizing the reliability of their products or the originality of the invention. At first all these pens were made of black hard rubber and looked very similar.

Soon, however, gold bands were added as adornment, and red and black mottled hard rubber was used as an alternative. Chasing was added to the rubber, then decorations came to include elegant twist patterns and, during the 1890s, gold and silver coverings with very attractive mother-of-pearl or abalone panels. With the minor exception of a very cheap pen made by the Eagle Pencil Co., which used a replaceable glass vial to contain the ink, all these early working pens had a hollow barrel that was filled with an eyedropper.

RIGHT **1910s 18-carat gold eyedropper pen; manufacturer unknown, but possibly Kaweco; 5½ inches. The fine and elegant artwork, depicting a horse and woman, has diamond chips inset on the outline. Although the pen is unsigned, it is so fine and extraordinarily well made that it is very valuable.**

BELOW **1899 eyedropper pen by Paul E. Wirt; 5½ inches. The cable and twist pattern of this gold-filled pen was one of the designs that pen manufacturers began to use in the early 1890s. The similarities between the metalwork found on pens made by different companies reveal how they used the same parts suppliers.**

BELOW **1899 eyedropper pen by Paul E. Wirt; 5¼ inches. The pen is decorated with a gold-filled repoussé pattern and has a repoussé taper cap. Wirt had patents dating back to 1873, more than a decade before Waterman, although no one seems to know what the patents were for. When Waterman was selling pens in the tens of thousands and Parker had only just started production in a back room, Wirt had already sold millions of pens.**

ABOVE **1896 Waterman no. 48; 7-inch desk pen. Although most no. 48 pens are retractors, for a short period the company used this number to designate a desk series. This example has the original cap with which it** was supplied. **As a convertible desk/pocket pen it predated the Parker Duofold by more than 20 years. The last number on the Waterman numbering system indicates the size of nib, and this pen is exceptionally rare because this size (8) was manufactured only for a brief period.**

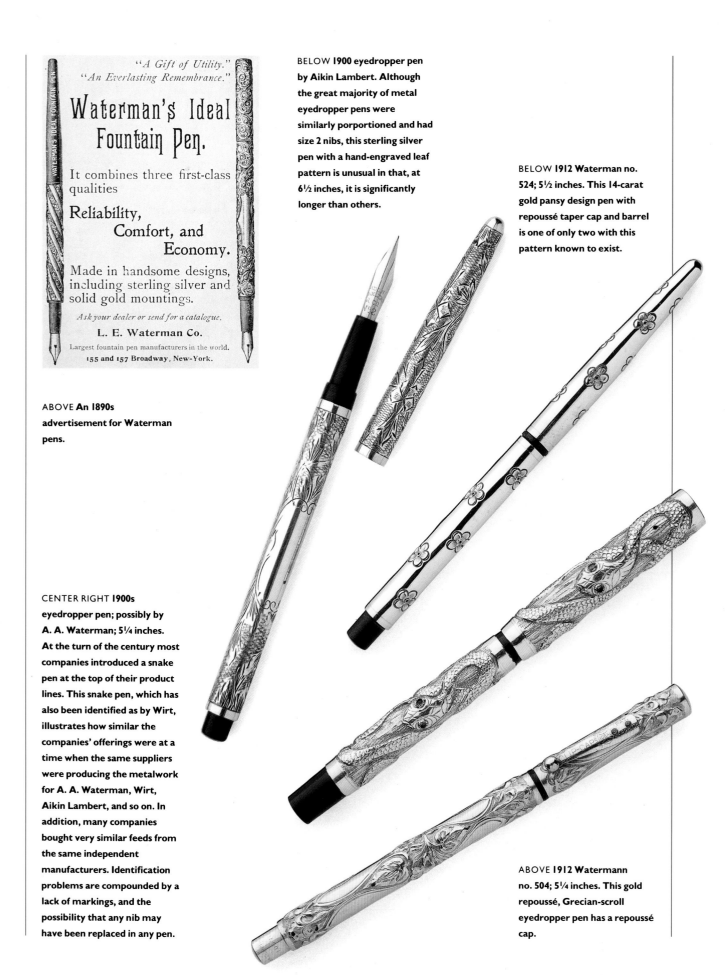

"A Gift of Utility."
"An Everlasting Remembrance."

Waterman's Ideal Fountain Pen.

It combines three first-class qualities

Reliability,
Comfort, and
Economy.

Made in handsome designs, including sterling silver and solid gold mountings.

Ask your dealer or send for a catalogue.

L. E. Waterman Co.

Largest fountain pen manufacturers in the world.
155 and 157 Broadway, New-York.

BELOW **1900 eyedropper pen by Aikin Lambert.** Although the great majority of metal eyedropper pens were similarly porportioned and had size 2 nibs, this sterling silver pen with a hand-engraved leaf pattern is unusual in that, at 6½ inches, it is significantly longer than others.

BELOW **1912 Waterman no. 524; 5½ inches.** This 14-carat gold pansy design pen with repoussé taper cap and barrel is one of only two with this pattern known to exist.

ABOVE **An 1890s** advertisement for **Waterman** pens.

CENTER RIGHT **1900s** eyedropper pen; possibly by **A. A. Waterman; 5¼ inches.** At the turn of the century most companies introduced a snake pen at the top of their product lines. This snake pen, which has also been identified as by Wirt, illustrates how similar the companies' offerings were at a time when the same suppliers were producing the metalwork for **A. A. Waterman, Wirt, Aikin Lambert,** and so on. In addition, many companies bought very similar feeds from the same independent manufacturers. Identification problems are compounded by a lack of markings, and the possibility that any nib may have been replaced in any pen.

ABOVE **1912 Watermann no. 504; 5¼ inches.** This gold repoussé, Grecian-scroll eyedropper pen has a repoussé cap.

RIGHT **1905 Waterman no. 404; 5¼ inches. This patch design, sterling silver eyedropper pen is extremely rare.**

ABOVE **1905 eyedropper pen by Parker; 5½ inches. The gold-filled, acid-etched scroll design is on an unusual background, and the artwork is uncataloged. There is a similar pen in the Parker Museum.**

ABOVE **A 1900s advertisement showing early Waterman fine silver filigree and black, chased hard rubber eyedropper models with chased, gold-filled bands.**

ABOVE **1905 eyedropper pen by Carey; 5½ inches. This sterling silver pen has highly repoussé floral work on the cap and barrel. These pens were produced in a variety of different motifs – acorns and figurines, for example – and they are exceptionally rare.**

ABOVE **1900s eyedropper pen by John Holland. The floral and leaf pattern is gold-filled repoussé. John Holland was a small regional company based in Cincinnati, which had produced dipping pens and nibs since the middle of the 19th century. Although it made the Mackinnon stylographic pen,** which was distributed worldwide, it went over to fountain pen production after the development of the channeled feed, although remaining a regional producer. While it may have developed the hatchet filler, probably as a means of circumventing Sheaffer or Waterman patents on levers, it produced no significant further developments after the 1920s.

RIGHT **1905 eye-dropper pen by Mabie, Todd & Bard; 5¼ inches.** A solid gold version of this elegant Swan gold-filled pen, with its twisted fluting and snail pattern chasing, is on permanent display in the Vatican Museum; it was presented as a personal gift to the then Pope by one of his congregations.

BELOW **1905 eyedropper pen by Mabie, Todd & Bard; 5¼ inches.** This Swan eyedropper model is in sterling silver and has rare holly-style chasing on the cap and barrel.

CENTER RIGHT **1900s eyedropper pen by Mabie, Todd & Bard; 5¼ inches.** The unusual design and construction of this sterling silver pen demonstrate that pen companies used a number of craftsmen to produce the decoration on their models. Neither the pen, the general design, nor the method of construction features in any catalog, but it is fully marked as being the product of the factory. Although it is common in collecting circles for particular pens to be identified as being the product of certain factories, and for certain pens to be identified as being produced by independent jewelers, it is doubtful that this classification has any real validity. The only really important points to look for are the quality of the workmanship and whether the artwork was factory commissioned. Pens such as the one shown here are more valuable in collectors' eyes because of their inherent rarity. However, subsequent poor quality, or modern additions by third parties, strongly affect value.

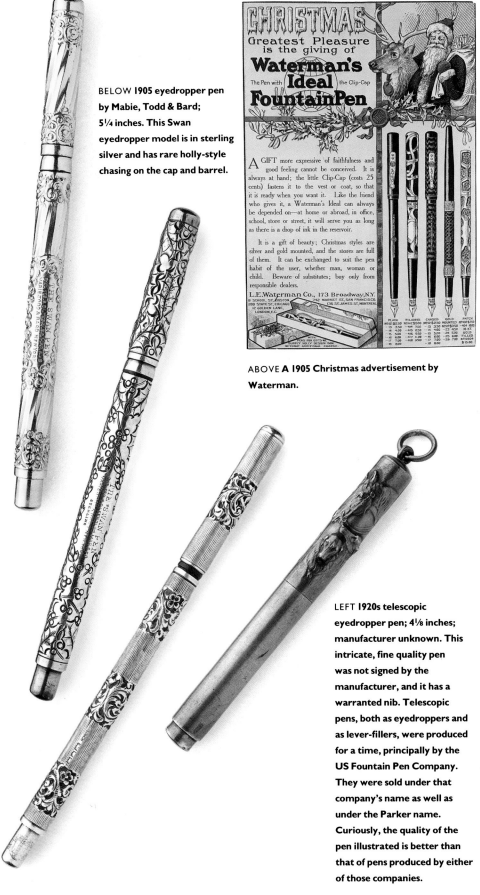

ABOVE **A 1905 Christmas advertisement by Waterman.**

LEFT **1920s telescopic eyedropper pen; 4⅛ inches; manufacturer unknown.** This intricate, fine quality pen was not signed by the manufacturer, and it has a warranted nib. Telescopic pens, both as eyedroppers and as lever-fillers, were produced for a time, principally by the US Fountain Pen Company. They were sold under that company's name as well as under the Parker name. Curiously, the quality of the pen illustrated is better than that of pens produced by either of those companies.

RIGHT **1912 eyedropper pen by Aikin Lambert; 5½ inches. This mother-of-pearl barreled pen combines the features of a taper cap and a unqiue scalloped design in the form of long troughs in each of the mother-of-pearl panels.**

BELOW **1911 Parker no. 47; 5½ inches. The abalone barrel of this highly sought-after pen has bulging panels, creating what is known as the "pregnant" effect. The cap has a gold-plated, repoussé floral design.**

LEFT *c.*1905 **Parker no. 15; 5¼ inches. The barrel is of alternating abalone and mother-of-pearl panels with an extremely unusual serrated pattern over black hard rubber, and the early rounded cap has a filigree design.**

RIGHT **1915 Waterman 414POC. The sterling silver overlay of this eyedropper pen has a "hand-hammered" effect.**

RIGHT **An exceptionally rare Eagle.**

BELOW **1903 Waterman no. 18; 6 inches.** This mottled, hard rubber, thimble-cap pen was a curious attempt to overcome the problem of ink leaking from the join between the barrel and the section in eyedropper pens by introducing a special section to cover the join. It was an extremely short-lived system, and examples are therefore rare, possibly because it is not clear what keeps the covering section on the barrel when the pen is being used and pressure is being exerted downwards on the barrel through that section.

LEFT **1905 crescent-filler by Conklin.** The red and black mottled, hard rubber crescent filler has a more normal locking ring and Van Valkenburgh clip.

ABOVE **1912 Waterman no. 18; 5⅗ inches.** This black, hard rubber safety pen is in the rare 8 nib size.

SAFETY PENS

In the United States, the L. E. Waterman Company had established a reputation as one of the foremost pen manufacturers by the 1900s. It did not, however, have in its range any self-filling pens whose patents it could readily utilize. The company's flirtations with the pump-filler in 1899 and 1903 proved particularly unsuccessful, the "pump" being nothing more than an adaptation of the idea first used by Parker in 1832 but married to a channeled feed.

By this time the US company Conklin, among others, was producing self-filling pens that appeared to be more technologically advanced than the available Waterman models. Waterman experimented with the production of a crescent-filler (presumably under some kind of short-lived licensing agreement with Conklin), but then concentrated on the production of the safety pen, using a spiral retractor mechanism. In these pens,

SPIRAL RETRACTOR MECHANISM

"In Fig. 78 (F. C. Brown, 1898, 8540), the nib, P, is held between the upper and lower tongues of the feed bar, H, which terminates in the form of a rod. A sleeve nut, S, is attached to the cap, K, and may be rotated by it. A pin in the rod, H, fits in the groove of the nut, S, and as the latter is rotated causes the rod, H, to travel in an upward or downward direction, as desired. The nib may thus be drawn within the nozzle, and the cap provided may then be screwed on at X, making a non-leakable joint." (Taken from *Journal of the Society of Arts*, Vol. LIII, No. 2, 764.)

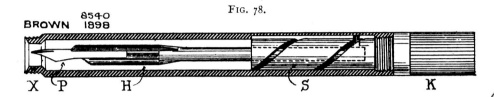

FIG. 78.

a spiral inside the barrel retracted the entire nib section into the barrel when the pen was not in use, and held it in the ink chamber. The primary advantage of this type of pen was that however it was treated, it would not leak because the barrel was effectively sealed in at both ends. The ink chamber formed almost the whole barrel, making the ink-holding capacity much larger than those pens with a rubber sack. In addition, because the nib sat in the ink reservoir and could not easily go dry, the pen was ready to write at the first stroke.

Having gone into production with a curious (and understandably rare) design using a slip-on cap that must have been blessed with few "safety" virtues, Waterman soon developed the threaded cap which caused the pens to operate in the way intended. Early examples may be identified by four or five raised threads, sometimes with an indent in the barrel to accommodate them. Soon, however, the threads lay flush with the barrel.

The first US pens to be imported into Europe were eyedropper models from Waterman and Mabie, Todd & Bard in the 1890s, but the retractor-type safety pen achieved great popularity throughout Europe in the 1910s. Their sales were further boosted by Waterman's publicity of David Lloyd George's use of one to sign the Treaty of Versailles after World War I.

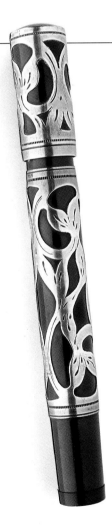

ABOVE **1913 Waterman no. 414; 5 inches.** This sterling silver safety pen is in the standard paisley design favored by most US manufacturers in the 1910s.

ABOVE **1905 safety pen by Moore.** This slender model has a repoussé sterling silver covering.

L. E. WATERMAN & CO. IN EUROPE

The retractable safety pen was the much copied design with which Waterman launched subsidiaries in France and Italy in the late 1910s, and although in the US Waterman had started to play down these retractor-type pens at a time it was introducing its new self-filling models, sales in France and Italy began with the safety pens. Although Waterman did market its simple eyedropper and self-filling pens in these countries, safety pens enjoyed the greatest sales. Waterman continued to sell large numbers of different models, some of exceptional beauty, in Italy well into the 1930s. Almost all of these were marked "18KR," indicating 18-carat rolled gold.

The problem for Waterman was not that other national producers were taking away sales in Italy, but that numerous manufacturers were copying not only Waterman designs but also the Waterman trademarks. The attitude of the company, whether it was the parent or local subsidiary, was ambivalent towards these infringements. Sometimes it sold the mechanical parts for production of safety pens to the local companies, and these pens are identified by the presence of the Waterman 42 number on the end of the barrel near the pin. Yet on other occasions it spent large amounts of money advertising that fakes were on the market and urging buyers to beware and buy only from Waterman dealers. They even went so far as to place a special seal on the "authorized" pens being sold through their own dealers in order to distinguish them from the copies. Soon, however, the copiers were copying the seals, and when different seals were introduced, these, too, were copied.

ABOVE **American mid-1930s advertisement for Waterman patrician pens.**

BELOW **1920s 18KR safety pen by Waterman; 5 inches; box 6 inches. The pierced and engraved design is in two colors, the crown has a decoration, and the clip is chased. The case is needlepoint.**

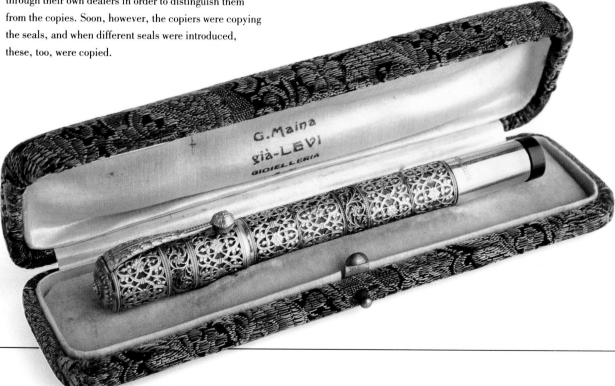

LEFT **1920 18KR safety pen by Waterman; 5 inches. The three-colored gold barrel over heavy longitudinal ribbing was made by Waterman's Italian subsidiary.**

ABOVE LEFT **1920S 18KR safety pen by Waterman; 5 inches. The two-tone spiral design is pierced and engraved, and there is a floral crown. An extraordinarily high quality of workmanship characterizes the products of Waterman's Italian subsidiary, with the artwork being mounted over hard rubber safety pen mechanisms that were produced in the US.**

FAR LEFT **Waterman marking on 18KR safety pens.**

ABOVE **1920s 18KR safety pen by Waterman 5 inches; casket-style box 6 inches. The pen is** decorated with pierced and engraved bands with chased decoration, and the floral crown has a chased clip. The semi-precious stone in the clip makes this pen even rarer and more desirable.

SAFETY PENS IN GERMANY

The German company Montblanc, which was then called the Simplo Filler Pen Company and selling pens under the name Rouge et Noir, sold eyedropper models for a brief period before standardizing its production around safety pens. These continued in production in various styles until the late 1930s. The company even designed its later series of safety pens (the 102–108 series) to look like more up-to-date self-filling models. Montblanc did make self-filling pens during the 1920s, including lever-fillers, blow-fillers, and pump-fillers, but these are very rare.

In Germany, the production of safety pens took two basic forms. Although there were no overtly conscious attempts to infringe US trademarks (and no US companies entered into litigation when their designs were copied), it was felt that pens would sell only if they were designed according to certain standard types. The major companies – Kaweco and Soennecken, for example – made the basic shape of their pens resemble Waterman's models, while most of the minor companies preferred to make their pens look like those made by Montblanc, with their distinctive milled band between the barrel and turning piece.

BELOW **1920 Montblanc no. 2; 4⅞ inches. This safety pen has an elegant pierced and engraved gold-filled barrel and cap. It was produced for Montblanc of Italy by local craftsmen, and is signed "Montblanc" on the cap. Although the presence of the** name confirms authenticity, German-made pens often do not bear any signature.

ABOVE **1922 safety pen by Goldfink; 4¾ inches. This German gold-filled pen was produced in Berlin by a company that is still in existence as a stationery company. Most of its pens had exceptionally flexible nibs, and were otherwise styled after Montblanc safety pens of the 1920s.**

BELOW **1920s safety pen; manufacturer unknown; box 3⅞ inches. The set is decorated in multicolored enameled silver over black hard rubber.**

IDENTIFICATION PROBLEMS

Although Montblanc usually marked all its standard hard rubber pens with its trademark or other identification, it is often possible to tell true Montblanc pens (especially metal ones, which were usually unmarked) only by the oval shape of the static pin that travels up and down the spiral inside the barrel. To complicate matters still further, Montblanc would make special pens, possibly for a store or even for another manufacturer such as Faber-Castell, that would be sold under another name and that would be specifically intended not to be identifiable as a Montblanc product. Such pens were sold under a wide variety of names, including Aladin, Clou, Diplomat, Gidania, Goldberg, Golding, Goldkopf, Helm, Hergo, Himmelfarb, Jemen, Kimmelstiel, Liberty, Monte Rosa, Omnibus, Pilot, Primaner, Quail, Royal, Simplo-Gold, Tatra, Thu-Wu, Ursus, and Westminster. These pens were often produced by the Excelsior Fountain Pen Company, which was set up in 1913 specifically for the purpose of producing Montblanc sub-brands.

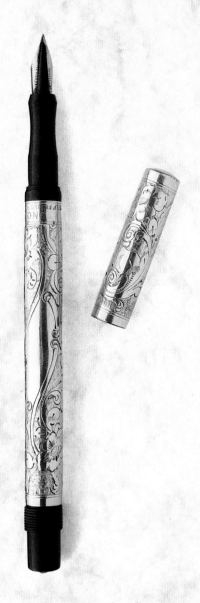

SELF-FILLING PENS

CHAPTER 2

At the turn of the century manufacturers' attention turned to refining the filling and reservoir systems, and two basic methods were adopted. One system used the barrel as a reservoir and concentrated on the use of a piston to create a vacuum inside it so that the barrel would be filled with ink when the vacuum was released into an ink bottle. This was the system used by the British firm De La Rue in the Onoto pen (see page 24).

The other system used a rubber sack inside the barrel to contain the ink, and some form of pressure bar to depress the sack while the nib was immersed in ink so that the ink could be drawn into the sack when the bar was released. Although it is not certain who first used a rubber sack to hold the ink, this method of filling was first applied commercially by Conklin of

TOP LEFT **1910 piston-filler by Onoto. A gold-plated, engraved model such as this would be keenly collected in Europe and Japan.**

ABOVE **A 1910s French advertisement for Onoto pens. De La Rue used the name Onoto because it could be assimilated into the greatest number of languages.**

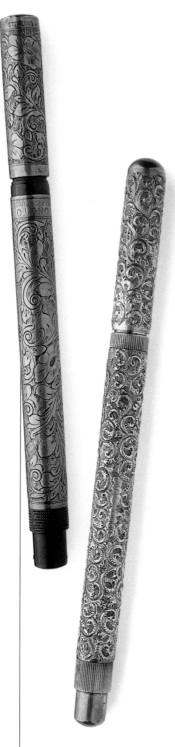

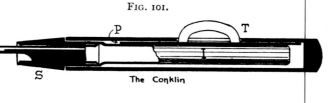

LEFT **The piston used on the Onoto.**

BELOW **1901 crescent filler by Conklin. It is a very early and exceptionally rare example of this model in gold; the locking ring is really just a ring that fits into the indentation in the crescent.**

Toledo, Ohio, with its crescent-filler; and by Crocker of Boston, Massachusetts, with its blow-filler.

In Conklin's pen, the crescent protruded from the side of the barrel, and a pressure bar was attached to its underside inside the barrel. A locking ring was rolled under the crescent to stop the pressure bar from pushing against the sack when the pen was not being filled. This method was copied all over the world, even after Conklin had abandoned the system, initially by Parker, with its click-filler; by Wirt, with a locking "hump"; and then by makers such as A. Nuñes, of Brazil and Portugal, and Spohr.

LEFT **1910 piston-filler by Onoto; 5¾ inches. These hand-engraved sterling silver models are particularly sought after in both Europe and Japan.**

RIGHT **1910 piston-filler by Onoto. This heavy repoussé sterling silver model is extremely desirable in Europe and Japan.**

THE CONKLIN

"The "Conklin" pen, shown in Fig. 101, is an improved form of the "Automatic" [sic]. Its method of refilling is precisely the same, but a pressure bar, P, is provided, which extends practically the entire length of the flexible ink container, I. When the thumb-piece, T, is pressed down the container, I, is flattened, and thus it is emptied of air. The casing of the pen is of vulcanite, and the point section, S, is fitted into it without any screw thread, as an ink tight joint is unnecessary. The ink-container may be readily and cheaply renewed when necessary, and for those who like a self-filling pen, this one ought to find favor." (Taken from *Journal of the Society of Arts*, Vol. LIII, No. 2, 764.)

FIG. 101.

P   T

S

The Conklin

BELOW **1910 crescent-filler by Conklin.** This gold-filled pen has a rare star pattern on the cap and barrel.

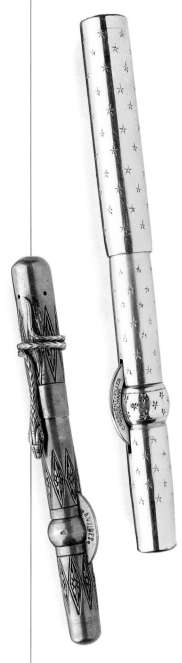

The
Sure-Welcome Gift

Conklin's
Self-Filling
Fountain Pen
NON-LEAKABLE

THE CONKLIN PEN MFG. CO.
291 Conklin Bldg., Toledo, Ohio, U.S.A.

ABOVE **A 1915 advertisement for Conklin's crescent-filler.** This advertisement shows that Conklin, in common with most other manufacturers, kept marketing the same designs for many years. All years of manufacture shown are necessarily therefore very imprecise.

ABOVE *c.***1910s crescent-filler by A. Nuñes; 4 inches.** This silver, Brazilian- or Portuguese-manufactured model is a copy of a Conklin pen. It is an unusual piece that features a platinum nib, a snake-type clip, and intricate engraving on the barrel and cap.

BELOW **1901 Taxon pen; 5⅜ inches.** This undistinguished pen from an otherwise unknown Philadelphia company has a button-style filler, which is released by turning the locking ring.

An intermediate system was the matchstick-filler, which was probably developed by an American company, Weidlich, or by Conklin. This system used a hole in the side of the barrel through which the user pushed a matchstick to press down the pressure bar. Weidlich's pens provided nonsmokers with an exceptionally inelegant matchstick sticking out of the end of the pen.

The sack-filling system developed chiefly from the early system used by Seth Crocker in the blow-filler fountain pen, which appeared *c.* 1901. This was a pen with a simple hole in the end of the barrel. To fill it, the nib was submerged in ink and the user blew through the hole into the barrel, thereby evacuating the air from the sack. When the sack reflated, air pressure caused the vacuum within the sack to be filled with ink. The cap also had a hole at the end, and the pen was so well made that a good seal was made when the cap was put on the end of the barrel. Thus the user's face did not need to be put too close to the ink bottle. In fact, a rubber ball was often supplied with the pen, and this could be attached to the barrel so that squeezing the ball expelled the air from the sack to create the necessary vacuum.

BELOW **1935 Zerolo by Omas; 5 inches. This burgundy and black pen has an unusual mechanism that spirals one nib out of the barrel while the other retracts. It is filled with a matchstick which is inserted into a hole in the barrel to depress a pressure bar that deflates one of the two rubber sacks, one behind each nib section.**

RIGHT **Zerolo Chameleon; 5½ inches.**

ABOVE **1925 suction-filler by Chilton. Early Chilton pens had curious cap/barrel proportions because it was thought necessary to cover the sliding outer section of the barrel with the cap when the pen was closed. In later pens the sliding section was designed to come out of the barrel end rather than the middle-barrel area. The pen illustrated has an elephant-skin finish.**

RIGHT **1904 Boston Safety Company. This pen is filled by means of a locking hump, much like the one in the Wirt pens.**

THE LEVER-FILLER

BELOW **Early Sheaffer lever.**

The major commercial problem facing most pen manufacturers in the first decades of the 20th century was the development by 1912 by the W. A. Sheaffer Pen Company of Fort Madison, Iowa, of the now familiar lever, which fitted flush with the barrel when it was not in use. It was simple, elegant, attractive, and easy to use. In addition, because the pen did not have to be dismantled before it could be filled, there was no danger of odd pieces being lost. The lever became the most widely used filling system for the next 40 years.

LEFT **1935 medium-size lever demonstrator by Sheaffer; 5½ inches. Sheaffer continued to use the lever largely unchanged from its invention until the 1940s. In the pen illustrated here the pressure bar is visible, as is the rubber sack, shown in white. Originally, the lever was attached with a short pin through the barrel. In the late 1920s, Sheaffer started to use a ring adhering to a channel inside the barrel, as shown here.**

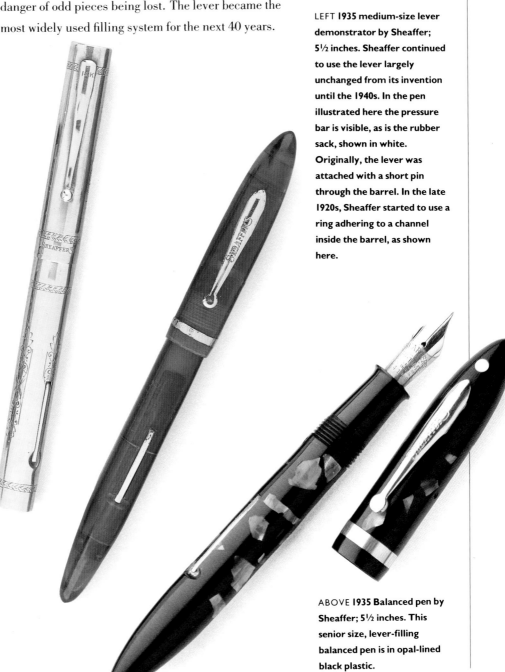

RIGHT **1920s Sheaffer no. 2; 4¾ inches. The rococo pattern on this pen has not been seen by authors of books on Sheaffer pens, even in catalogs.**

ABOVE **1935 Balanced pen by Sheaffer; 5½ inches. This senior size, lever-filling balanced pen is in opal-lined black plastic.**

L. E. Waterman, Parker, and Swan all experienced considerable difficulty in competing with the lever-filler. In the early 1910s they were still promoting the eyedropper system, and were rapidly losing sales to Sheaffer. It was essential that they found self-filling systems of their own – and preferably ones that actually worked, unlike Waterman's short-lived 1895 pump-filling system.

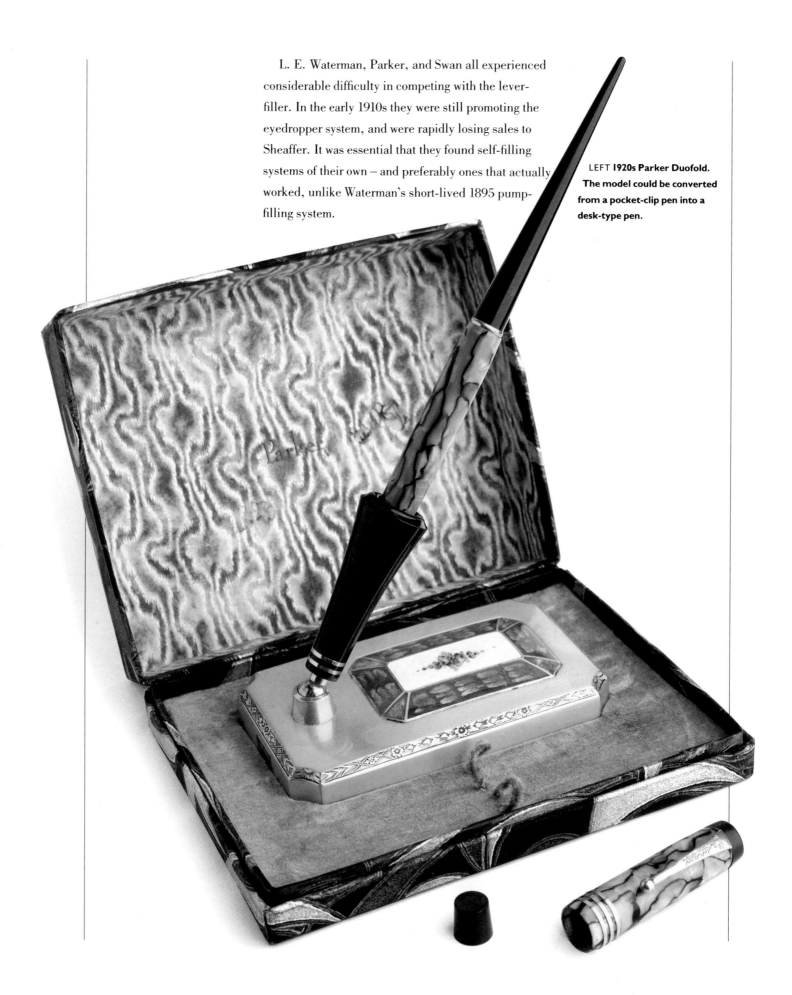

LEFT **1920s Parker Duofold. The model could be converted from a pocket-clip pen into a desk-type pen.**

Parker was slow to adapt to technological change, and did not feel the need to consider self-filling pens until forced to do so by Sheaffer's success. In 1904 Parker had patented the button-filler. In this, a button under a blind cap at the end of the barrel exerted longitudinal pressure on a sprung pressure bar within the barrel, which caused the bar to spring into the sack. This was the method Parker used for its famous Duofold range, which was so called because originally the blind cap was interchangeable with a long, thin continuation of the barrel, cleverly converting the pocket pen into a desk pen.

BELOW **1914 Waterman no. 14PSF. The coin-filler was another unsuccessful design produced when Waterman was attempting to find a self-filler to compete with Sheaffer's lever filler. It was produced for a year only and is exceptionally rare, especially in a filigree design of the kind shown here.**

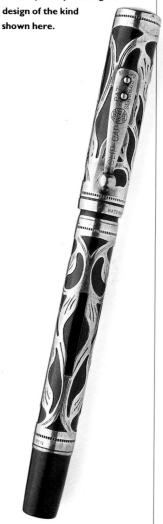

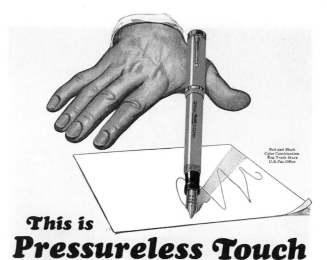

This is Pressureless Touch

$7 and $5 *according to size*
There is no reason today to pay more than Parker Prices for a fountain pen. You can't buy more than DUOFOLD EFFICIENCY which will last you all your life.

This pen's feather-light weight alone is sufficient to start it writing instantly and keep it writing. Scarcely any pressure from your fingers, no effort, no fatigue. You simply guide this pen.

Doubly remarkable is this improvement, because the new Duofold is 28% lighter in weight than when made with rubber. Now we are using Parker Permanite, a material. This pen, therefore, is one of the lightest writing instruments we know.

And while making the pen lighter, this material has made it Non-Breakable also. We have thrown these new Duofolds from an aeroplane 3,000 feet aloft and not one has broken.

But Pressureless Touch is most important because of its effect of taking all the effort out of writing. It clears the track for THINKING as no other feature in a fountain pen has ever done before.

Five smart colors—Lacquer-red, Lapis Lazuli Blue, Green Jade, Imperial Mandarin Yellow [new] and flashing Black and Gold—all black-tipped. Duofold Pencils to match.

Three sizes of pen barrels—the Over-size, the Junior and the slender Lady Duofold, each offering six styles of pen points tempered to yield to any hand but proof against distortion from the shape you like.

Get all these Parker features by being sure to look for "Geo. S. Parker—DUOFOLD," imprinted on each pen or pencil. Don't let color only be your guide.

THE PARKER PEN COMPANY, JANESVILLE, WIS.
OFFICES AND SUBSIDIARIES:
NEW YORK · BOSTON · CHICAGO · ATLANTA
DALLAS · SAN FRANCISCO
TORONTO, CANADA · LONDON, ENGLAND

The Permanent Pen

Parker Duofold OVER-SIZE **$7**
Duofold Jr., $5   Lady Duofold, $5

Parker Duofold Pencils to match Duofold Pens. The lead turns out for writing, in for carrying. $3, $3.50 and $4.

Red and Black Color Combination Reg. Trade Mark U.S. Pat. Office

ABOVE **1927 Parker Duofold Senior; 5½ inches. This button-filler is in black and pearl.**

ABOVE **A 1927 advertisement for the Parker Mandarin Yellow Duofold, a pen that George Parker produced after being entranced with the color during a trip to China.** **It never sold well and is rare – and desirable – today. The material has not held up well over time and is relatively brittle, tending to crack, especially around the cap lip.**

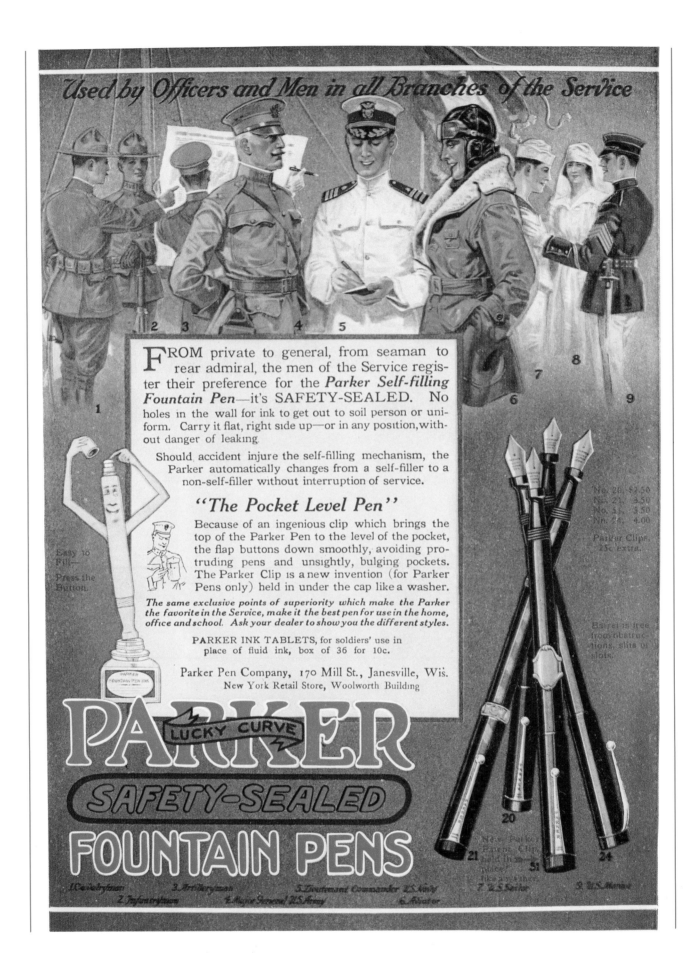

Used by Officers and Men in all Branches of the Service

FROM private to general, from seaman to rear admiral, the men of the Service register their preference for the *Parker Self-filling Fountain Pen*—it's SAFETY-SEALED. No holes in the wall for ink to get out to soil person or uniform. Carry it flat, right side up—or in any position, without danger of leaking.

Should accident injure the self-filling mechanism, the Parker automatically changes from a self-filler to a non-self-filler without interruption of service.

"The Pocket Level Pen"

Because of an ingenious clip which brings the top of the Parker Pen to the level of the pocket, the flap buttons down smoothly, avoiding protruding pens and unsightly, bulging pockets. The Parker Clip is a new invention (for Parker Pens only) held in under the cap like a washer.

The same exclusive points of superiority which make the Parker the favorite in the Service, make it the best pen for use in the home, office and school. Ask your dealer to show you the different styles.

PARKER INK TABLETS, for soldiers' use in place of fluid ink, box of 36 for 10c.

Parker Pen Company, 170 Mill St., Janesville, Wis.
New York Retail Store, Woolworth Building

Easy to Fill—
Press the Button.

No. 20, $2.50
No. 21, 3.50
No. 51, 3.50
No. 24, 4.00

Parker Clips, 25c extra.

Barrel as free from obstructions, slits or slots.

PARKER
LUCKY CURVE
SAFETY-SEALED
FOUNTAIN PENS

20
21
51
24

1. Cavalryman   3. Artilleryman   5. Lieutenant Commander U.S. Navy   7. U.S. Sailor   9. U.S. Marine
2. Infantryman   4. Major General U.S. Army   6. Aviator

LEFT **A 1917 advertisement for Parker's button-filler system.**

L. E. Waterman tried several different systems – the coin-filler, which was a matchstick-type system using a coin; the sleeve-filler, which was probably initially developed by Century or Aikin Lambert and in which a sleeve moved along the barrel to reveal a pressure bar that was depressed with a finger; and the simple suction-pump filler – before alighting on its own lever housed within a box section, which apparently did not infringe Sheaffer's patents.

LEFT **1914 Waterman no. 0515. This plain sleeve-filler pen is gold-filled. The illustration shows the rear of the barrel.**

LEFT **1910s sleeve-filler by Aikin Lambert. The illustration shows the section around the barrel which rotates. When it is in the "closed" position, the barrel interior is often plain and can be used for initials. The pen illustrated is decorated with gold-filled chasing.**

ABOVE **1910s sleeve-filler by Century; 5½ inches. In this pen, which is decorated with a ribbon-style, gold-filled filigree, the whole barrel is rotated to reveal the pressure bar.**

LEFT **1915 Waterman no. 412SF. This filigree sleeve-filler is an extremely desirable pen.**

RIGHT **1914 Waterman no. 0512PSF. The long, thin barrel of this filigree pump-filler housed the pump mechanicals in the end. This was another unsuccessful design produced when Waterman was attempting to find a self-filler to compete with Sheaffer's lever-filler. It was produced for only a year and is exceptionally rare, especially in a filigree design.**

ABOVE **A sterling silver repoussé pen by Perry; 6 inches. It is similar to the Post, having the same piston.**

CENTER LEFT **Early 1900s piston-filler pens. The black hard rubber Post accounting pen, 4⅞ inches assembled, is marked "WHS" (probably indicating the retailer). This was the early piston system that resembled a syringe in operation. Like the 1890s Waterman pump-filler (7¼ inches), it seems to have been based on a marriage between John Jacob Parker's 1832 system and the channeled feed. Later developments, especially by Pelikan in the late 1920s, involved enlarging the ink supply from under a half to almost the whole barrel by making the puller a telescopic twist mechanism.**

LEFT **1905 pull-filler by John Holland; 4¼ inches. This early system, which was devised by the Cincinnati company, involved collapsing the sack by pulling on a "saddle" outside the barrel. The price sticker that is still on barrel indicates that this pen is "new old stock" – that is, it was never sold by the original retailer.**

1894 POST

"The body, A, of the pen shown in Fig. 53 W. Post, 1894, (1039), contains a plunger or piston, E, attached to a rod or handle, F. The nib, C, fits into grooves in the point section, B. The body, or reservoir, A, is filled with ink by operating the plunger, E. The original pen as described in the patent specification, shows the rod, F, as one piece, but the pen as now made has a telescopic rod, which reduces the length of the complete pen." (Taken from *Journal of the Society of Arts*, Vol. LIII, No. 2, 763.)

FIG. 53.

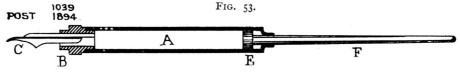

POST 1039 1894

FOUNTAIN PENS IN JAPAN

The evolution of pens in Japan differed from European and US developments. Although the Japanese used safety pens, they were relatively slow to adopt fountain pens, probably because the complex Kanji characters (the Japanese system of writing using Chinese characters) require a soft, fine, and extremely flexible medium, traditionally a brush. It was relatively difficult to write Kanji characters with early fountain pens, which tended either not to write at all or to leak or cause blots when they were held upright to form the characters.

The situation remained unchanged until the early years of the 20th century, when Thomas De La Rue introduced the Onoto piston-filling pen into Japan. The pens were called Onoto principally because the word could be easily assimilated into a large number of languages, and De La Rue marketed them all over the world. The filling system had been invented, apparently in his spare time, by a George Sweetser, whose full-time profession was a vaudeville performer doing a transvestite act on rollerskates. The pen was exceptionally successful in Japan, and it was one of the few types of pen – certainly one of the few foreign-made pens – to be sold there in 1900–20. Its success may have been due to the fact that the Japanese thought that the manufacturer was local, but,

whatever the reason, it proved so popular that it achieved almost mythic status, and even today the word Onoto in Japan will give rise to the same connotations as Rolls-Royce or Aston Martin.

When Japanese fountain pen companies began production, therefore, they felt that the pens would be successful only if they resembled the Onoto, with its distinctive internal plunger-filling system. So that they did not copy the De La Rue model too closely, local manufacturers developed their own version of the Onoto valve. Although this looked like a normal piston, it was in fact an eyedropper with a valve in the barrel above the section that touched the rear of the feed, as in the early Onoto pens. When this valve pushed against the feed, it closed off the ink supply to the feed, and in order to get the pen to write the piston had to be withdrawn slightly from the feed. This was achieved, in the same way as in the early Onoto pens, by giving the blind cap at the end of the barrel a half-turn.

When these pens are found today, many collectors fail to realize that the only function of the piston is to start the ink flow and that, in other respects, these are simple eyedropper-fillers. It is often assumed that the piston is part of a filling system that is not working.

TOP 1910 eyedropper-filler by Swan (of Japan); 5 inches. This company had no relationship whatsoever with the Anglo-American company also called Swan, which was owned by Mabie, Todd. However, the Japanese company registered its name in Japan before Mabie, Todd tried to do so, thereby effectively shutting its namesake out of the Japanese market. The company exists today and continues to produce fountain pens.

BELOW LEFT 1930s ink-flow valve eyedropper pen; Japanese. The handpainted tiger decoration over heavy gold dust was signed by the artist. Japanese hand-lacquered pens are generally the exception to the rule that pens that do not bear the manufacturer's name are of significantly lower value than those that are so marked. This large pen – around a size 6 nib – is of the highest quality and has obviously been made and painted in a grade equal to that of the Namiki factory, possibly by someone who had been trained there. During the 1930s, many individual craftsmen practised this particular art in a cottage-industry fashion.

THE SUCTION-FILLER

By the mid-1920s, the disadvantages of having to blow into a sack to fill a pen were apparent, and companies began to experiment with designs to compete with the lever system that so many manufacturers had adopted. Crocker used a hatchet-filler, which resembled a reverse lever, swinging around outside the barrel to apply backward pressure on the pressure bar in exactly the same way as the more conventional lever design. The system had no obvious advantages, and seems to have been introduced solely to get around the lever patents.

By 1925 Chilton, an American company run by Seth Crocker's son, had refined the design of the suction-filler by developing a sealed tube, which was outside the barrel, but retaining the hole at the end that Crocker had used. By sliding the exterior tube back, covering the hole, and pushing the tube back into position, air was expelled from the sack. The pen was then placed in the ink, and the sack filled on reflation.

At first these pens were relatively ungainly, largely because the pen was developed around the mechanism. The join at the end of the exterior tube was put halfway up the barrel, supposedly for convenience, and the cap was designed in such a way that it met the join. The pens had a different balance from any other type of pen, and they looked very distinctive, with the cap being relatively long in terms of the overall closed length. After a while Chilton began to use pens that had a more normal proportion of cap to barrel, and during the mid-1930s the company's Wing Flow pens (which were decorated with inlaid metalwork) were among the most beautiful models to be produced.

BELOW LEFT **An Aurora-Edacoto hatchet-filler with an art deco band; 5¼ inches.**

BELOW RIGHT **1936 wing-flow suction-filler by Chilton. These enchanting pens featured inlaid gold-filled metalwork. The pen shown is cherry red.**

CHILTON – THE LATER YEARS

Unfortunately, Chilton was nearing the end of its lifecycle, and was struggling against the economic downturn affecting most pen manufacturers. The Wing Flow nib was really an indicator of the company's plight. Although it was publicized as a clever method of preventing the nib from moving around in the section, in reality it was a means by which the company could reduce the amount of precious metal in the nib. The nib wrapped around the feed only because it was not long enough to go sufficiently far into the section to be secured in place. In addition, the gold was so thin that nib cracking is a major problem with Chilton pens dating from the mid-1930s. Nevertheless, the company continued to produce stylish pens into the 1940s, and remained true to the original suction-fill principle.

THE PISTON-FILLER

Development of the suction-fill system came from an unlikely quarter. During the 1930s, pen companies felt it necessary to introduce more complex filling systems, and for some hitherto unexplained reason Sheaffer, Omas, and Eversharp managed to make their pens more complex by abandoning the lever. First, they introduced an Onoto-type piston-filling system, designed around a thin metal shaft and piston. Then they developed the Chilton system by dropping the piston and putting a sack into a version of the piston-filler.

Most of these thick shaft mechanisms are found in the Sheaffer Snorkel pen, which was mass-produced during the 1940s. The Snorkel pen may be easily identified by the thin tube that screws out of the center of the feed under the hooded nib. This was felt to be a major advantage when it was introduced because the snorkel tube was extended before the pen was filled, and it was the tube, not the whole nib section, that was dipped into the ink. The plunger was depressed and the pen filled without the nib coming into contact with the ink. When the filling process was concluded and the pen removed from the ink bottle, the snorkel would be retracted into the feed to lie flush with it. It was not, therefore, necessary to wipe excess ink off the nib after filling.

However, although Sheaffer may have adopted the piston system because the ink capacity was increased when the whole barrel was used to hold ink rather than the sack used with the lever-filler, the snorkel system reduced the ink-holding capacity very considerably. Possibly in line with current fashion, the pen was thin, and the barrel had to hold a spring that went around the stainless steel tube that held the sack. There was, therefore, limited room for the sack itself, let alone ink within the sack.

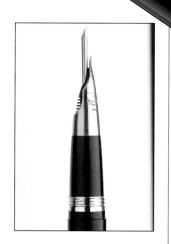

PISTON/SHAFT-FILLERS

These pens can be distinguished by the central tube: if it is a thin, stainless steel shaft the pen is a piston-filler; if the shaft is thick, it is a sack-type filler (the shaft has to be thick to hold the sack).

BELOW Thin Sheaffer shaft.   BELOW Snorkel shaft.

ABOVE **1940s Sheaffer Snorkel; 5⅝ inches. Mass-produced during the 1940s and 1950s, this pen is often found by collectors. It may be identified by the small tube that emerges from the underside of the hooded nib. Although it was very well made by a company that did not compromise on quality, even when the right materials were difficult to find, its mechanism was so complex that there was little room for the ink supply.**

ABOVE **Snorkel.**

ZEROLO PENS

The matchstick-filler system was revived by Omas during the 1930s with the Zerolo which had two separate nibs, sections, and sack chambers within the barrel so that either two colors of ink could be used or (less commonly) two types of nib could be accommodated within one pen. One side spiraled out of the barrel, while the other spiraled back into the barrel as the end was turned, a feature reminiscent of the safety pens. Because there was no space within the barrel for levers or filling mechanisms, a simple hole was inserted in the side of the barrel so that the pressure bar (which was integral with the sack chamber) could be pushed. The matchstick unscrewed from under the blind cap above the clip. Because of the complexity of the mechanism, combined with the difficulty of synchronizing the movement of the two nib sections and aligning them with the hole so that the matchstick could marry with the pressure bar, replacing the sacks in a Zerolo should not be attempted by a novice.

MATERIALS

Pen manufacturers had always been using black hard rubber. From the earliest stages they also used red (or very rarely green) and black mottled hard rubber. At around the time of World War I, they began to use hard rubber with more complicated woodgrain and, later, ripple patterns as well as hard rubber in bright red. These patterns and colors continued to be used until the mid-1920s, when plastic was introduced and a wide range of colors became available. Combinations of colors became common – black and pearl was especially popular – and different designs, including striations, were used.

BELOW **A 1920s security check protector; 5¾ inches. This unusual cap arrangement contained an inked wheel with serrated edges which was immediately rolled over a signature, and presumably the amount, on a check to prevent later alteration.**

LEFT **1925 Wahl-Eversharp; 5⅜ inches. This medium-size lever-filler is in "rosewood."**

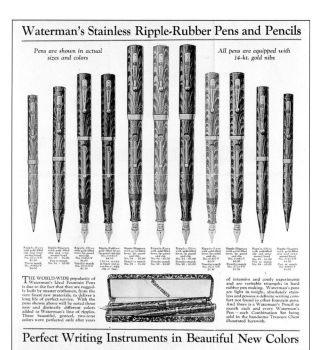

Waterman's Stainless Ripple-Rubber Pens and Pencils

Pens are shown in actual sizes and colors

All pens are equipped with 14-kt. gold nibs

Perfect Writing Instruments in Beautiful New Colors

LEFT **A late-1920s advertisement for the Waterman no. 94 series ripple pen.**

BELOW **Late 1920s Parker Duofold Petite pens in pastel-colored Permanite; 5¼ inches. These pastel colors were available only in this size.**

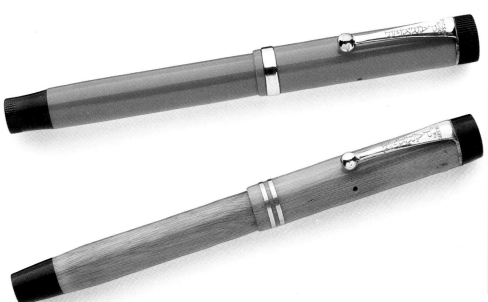

ABOVE **1920s Waterman no. 58; 6 inches. Although attempts were made to match the patterns on caps and barrels on the production line, this pen shows slight differences in the ripple. The top of the cap is black ripple over red, while the bottom of the barrel is red ripple over black. Some pens have even been found that are ripple at one end, match at the barrel/cap intersection, and become woodgrain at the other end.**

LEFT **1920s Tortoise lever-filler; 5¼ inches.** This pen, of which only one example has been found and which was manufactured by an otherwise unknown company, was made entirely of tortoiseshell which was popular in Britain during the first half of the 20th century. The pen has very high quality solid gold trim, which seems to resemble the Conway Stewart style, but its markings resemble Japanese copies of the Waterman Ideal Globe.

ABOVE **Early 1930s Swan no. 2 Eternal in green-lined black plastic; 5¼ inches.**

ABOVE **1930s Conklin Symmetrik; senior size.** This jade green, black-veined pen is a lever-filler.

ABOVE **Early 1930s Swan no. 2 Eternal in coral plastic.**

LEFT **Early 1930s Monroe; senior size.** The art deco-style stepped cap and barrel ends made this relatively undistinguised pen stand out in the crowd.

This white dot identifies Sheaffer's, the ONLY genuine Lifetime° pen.

BALANCE
The only Balance° pen and pencil is Sheaffer's.

Golf, No. HGR, $3

Petite, No. H74MC, $7.75

Golf, No. KGR, $3

Medium, No. KTSC, $4

Petite, No. HMC, $3.50

Medium, No. K74TC, $9.50

New! Petite Lifetimes.° Small! Smart! For school, business, social writing

Unique? Yes! The new vogue in line and color? Indeed! Is that all? By no means! The clever little Petite Balance° Lifetimes° also are most practical. Perfect Balance° is engineered into them, they are scientifically moulded and proportioned to cut bulk and put weight and length just where they're wanted, and so they write airily, handle comfortably, and slip neatly into handbag or pocket. Choose the one of the fifteen pen points that suits your hand, sense the fluency of Balance° writing, realize that this fine instrument is guaranteed to serve loyally for your lifespan—and you'll want Petite Lifetimes°!

AT BETTER STORES EVERYWHERE

The ONLY genuine Lifetime° pen is Sheaffer's; do not be deceived! All pens are guaranteed against defect, but Sheaffer's Lifetime° is guaranteed unconditionally against everything excepting loss for your lifetime. Jade Green and Jet Black Lifetime° pens, $8.75; Ladies', $8.25. Marine Green and Black-and-Pearl De Luxe, $10; Ladies', $9.50. Petite Lifetime° pens, $7 up. Pencils, $5. Others lower.

SHEAFFER'S
PENS·PENCILS·DESK SETS·SKRIP

W. A. SHEAFFER PEN COMPANY · FORT MADISON, IOWA, U. S. A.
New York   Chicago   San Francisco
W. A. Sheaffer Pen Co. of Canada, Ltd.   169-173 Fleet St., Toronto, Ont.
Wellington, N. Z.   Sydney, Australia   London, Eng.
° Reg. U. S. Pat. Off.
© W. A. S. P. Co., 1930

SAFETY SKRIP, SUCCESSOR TO INK SKRIP-FILLED, 50c TO $10. Every literate person between the ages of five and one hundred should have a package of Safety Skrip —saves furniture, rugs, clothing, keeps the fluid fresh, makes all pens write better.

ABOVE **Mid-1930s advertisement for Sheaffer's lever-filling, balanced.**

LEFT 1935 Parker Vacumatic; 4¾ inches. Medium size, in green shadow-wave pattern.

RIGHT 1933 button-filler by Parker. This button-filler, which dates from the years of the Depression, is in an unusual blue and onyx-lined golden color. In general, Parker did not buy from the central plastic-producing combine for its major models, but this less expensive model was made in a plastic that is often found in the products of many other pen manufacturers. It was not marketed widely.

LEFT AND BELOW 1935 Carter; 5¼ inches; medium size; set in black with lime green veining.

RIGHT Early 1930s lever-filler by Conklin; junior size. This Endura was made in a tiger-tail pattern of red/orange/white/ black.

LEFT 1932 lever-filler by Wahl-Eversharp; senior size. The green and bronze pen is decorated with an art deco patterned band.

A number of companies tried a variety of other materials. In the late 1910s, for example, LeBoeuf, of Springfield, Massachusetts, experimented with cellulose nitrate (known as Celluloid by Dupont, its main manufacturer), but few other manufacturers used this highly inflammable substance before the 1920s. A few companies tried casein, a milk-based product, but this never really caught on largely because it tended to degrade or break. Casein absorbs moisture and swells then contracts when it dries, and cracks often appeared when this happened. During the 1920s, companies turned to Celluloid and its derivatives in larger numbers. Sheaffer called it Radite; Parker knew it as Permanite; Wahl-Eversharp and others referred to it as Pyralin. Montblanc used Bayer Celluloid.

BELOW **1929 celluloid LeBoeuf no. 8; 5½ inches. A gray pearl, translucent sleeve-filler.**

ABOVE **1927 celluloid LeBoeuf no. 8; 5½ inches. LeBoeuf, which produced this tigereye lever-filler, was probably the first company to experiment with Celluloid, sometime after 1919. It was able to do so because it had patented a method of manufacturing pens out of tubing; the end was either plugged or had a screw-in blind cap. The colors used were, therefore, completely different from those found in other manufacturers' models.**

RIGHT **1927 celluloid LeBoeuf no. 8; 5½ inches. A gray swirl lever-filler.**

ABOVE **1935 Sheaffer, senior size; 5½ inches. A lever-filling, balanced pen in red-veined gray and black marbled plastic.**

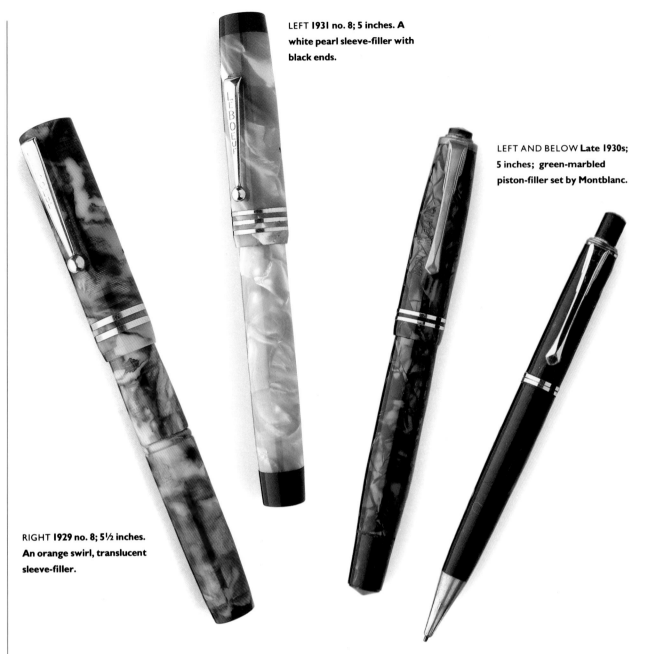

LEFT **1931 no. 8; 5 inches. A white pearl sleeve-filler with black ends.**

LEFT AND BELOW **Late 1930s; 5 inches; green-marbled piston-filler set by Montblanc.**

RIGHT **1929 no. 8; 5½ inches. An orange swirl, translucent sleeve-filler.**

At first the major manufacturers ordered the whole production run of a certain type of plastic so that they could have exclusive use of a particular color. It is possible to identify the manufacturers of pens made in the 1920s with some degree of certainty merely by looking at the type of plastic used. During the 1930s, the position got more complicated. The Depression meant that pen manufacturers could no longer easily afford to hold large stocks of the plastics they needed. When the rod stock had been made, the plastic had to be allowed to cure for a considerable time before it could be drilled to make the caps and barrels. Few

BELOW **1930s pen/pencil combination by Conklin. These were popular as curiosities for a short period during the 1930s, and they were made by most US manufacturers. They were not in production for long, however, because it was soon found that they had neither a great ink capacity, nor a** particularly large lead supply. In addition the public found them ugly. Large numbers of poor-quality examples may be found in flea markets today, and gold or gold-filled examples are found in jewelers' stocks of unsaleable merchandise.

LEFT **1927 Stilus; 4⅝ inches. This Italian pen was modeled on the Duofold Junior.**

ABOVE **1929 no. 8; 5 inches. A unique purple and black pearl with black ends.**

LEFT **1935 Extra Lucens by Omas; 5¼ inches. A gray and pearl, three-band, round pen. The pen was called Lucens because light showed through the barrel to reveal the ink inside.**

RIGHT **Olo; 5¼ inches. White with brown stripes.**

companies wanted to finance the holding of large stocks, especially if the rods could not be used immediately. This situation led to a cooperative being formed in the US to order and hold the stocks so that the companies could buy the plastic as and when they needed it.

With few exceptions – notably Sheaffer, which used its own rod stock and developed a technique to stabilize it quickly after manufacture – the same plastics can therefore be found on pens coming from several makers. As an example, all the plastics used in the expensive Waterman Patrician can be found in the relatively inexpensive Parker pens produced at the time of the Depression. Occasionally even companies such as LeBoeuf, which made the highest quality fountain pens, used plastics that were common to companies such as Morrison, which produced low quality pens. Although this did not apply to the materials that were made from compressed layered sheeting, such as the material used by Parker in its Vacumatics, the cooperative use of materials was not confined to the US. The supposedly exclusive Bayer Celluloid, much publicized in the 1930s by Montblanc for its rare and desirable Platinum Lined (PL) series, can also be found in the very valuable Omas Extra Lucens from the same period.

RIGHT **Zemax; 5 inches. With an orange art deco-style band.**

RIGHT **Tabo; 5½ inches. This Parker Vacumatic look-alike was made in Bologna in the 1930s.**

ABOVE **Caesar Extra; 4¾ inches.**

LEFT **Montegrappa;
5¼ inches. A streamlined red
lever-filler.**

LEFT AND BELOW **1940
Ancora; 5¼ inches. This
streamlined red pen with a clip
is similar to the first year's
production of Waterman's
"100-year pen."**

BELOW **1936 Montblanc no.
128PL. The largest of the rare
and highly desirable Montblanc
Platinum Lined series, this
twist-filler was made of a
special Celluloid which was
produced by Bayer and which
was advertised as being
exclusive to Montblanc. It was,
however, also used by Omas,
among other companies.**

BELOW **Extra Lucens by Omas;
5¼ inches. Omas produced a
Platinum Lined series, similar
to the Montblanc pens.**

ABOVE **1934 no. 8 by Eugene
LeBoeuf; 5 inches. Holy water
asperge in gray and pearl.**

MASS-PRODUCED PENS

As the 1930s progressed and the Depression took its toll, companies began to look for ways of mass-producing pens that were preferably both cheaper and more technologically advanced than those of their competitors. In general these developments offered few significant advances over their predecessors, being introduced chiefly for fashion or marketing purposes. It was felt, for example, that an ink shut-off would reduce the possibility of ink leakage, especially in the pressurized air conditions found in aircraft. This ignored the fact that the recently discontinued safety pens made by, among others, Waterman, Moore and Montblanc contained a sealed ink chamber that would not leak under extreme conditions. Complex ink shut-off mechanisms were developed and offered as advances over the competition. These did not work, and soon the companies producing them were forced to stop claiming that they did. Safety pens continued in production, and Waterman had to reintroduce its model for aircraft use. Waterman of France had never stopped selling safety pens, and it was relatively easy to rename its old designs Aero-Waterman.

ABOVE **Ink shut off.**

BELOW **Mid-1930s Gold Bond plunger-filler; 4¾ inches. This inexpensive pen was produced to satisfy a 1930s fad for pens with ink shut-off mechanisms, which can be seen as a spring mounted above the nib. These systems were intended to prevent ink leaking in non-pressurized aircraft, but they did not work and (especially in the case of Wahl-Eversharp) the companies producing them were forced by the US Federal Trade Commission to stop claiming that they did.**

CARTRIDGE PENS

Waterman of France had developed a cartridge pen as early as 1927, but it had not promoted it either at home or abroad. The company adapted its design from the old removable glass vial system used in the 1890s by Eagle in its inexpensive pens. Although it has been claimed that 1927 heralded the "modern age" of fountain pens, the cartridge did not become popular until the mid-1960s, and early French examples with glass cartridges are rare.

RIGHT **1930 Ibis; 4½ inches.**
Pelikan also used the twist-filler system in its more upmarket Ibis line. During the 1930s, Jews who wanted to escape the Nazi regime in Germany could take with them only a limited range of goods, and for some reason fountain pens were permitted. A large number, therefore, found their way to Israel and to South America, although because of the instability of the plastic material, not many have survived.

LEFT **Transparent section.**

ABOVE **1939 Vacumatic Maxima; silver with striations.**

ABOVE **Vacumatic plunger.**

Another perceived advantage was to have a transparent area in the barrel through which the ink level could be seen. The problem was that it was difficult to have a transparent section of the barrel near a rubber sack – all that would be seen would be the black sack, for as yet no manufacturer had developed a translucent or transparent sack. Sheaffer and Eversharp went to great lengths to insert transparent sections between the area behind the nib and the barrel threads although the plastics used were simply not sufficiently sophisticated to successfully execute the ingenious ideas of the pen designers.

Parker tried a different system with its Vacumatic. It replaced the sack with a rubber diaphragm at the end of the barrel, and introduced complex mechanisms to hold the diaphragm in place and use it to suck up ink. The material used by Parker was compressed layered sheeting, and alternate layers could be transparent, to give a semi-transparent effect to the whole while retaining the strength of the colored material.

Eventually most of these mechanisms were discarded and manufacturers returned to the old systems, although they promoted them as technological breakthroughs. In the late 1930s, the Italian company Aurora found that it had to reintroduce the eyedropper-filler, ostensibly as a convenience for Italian soldiers who needed a reliable pen for use in the trenches. This was similar to the models produced by Waterman, Moore, Parker, and Swan during World War I. Aurora's pen was an eyedropper-filler with a compartment in the barrel end that contained ink pellets. The pellets were inserted into the barrel, which was filled with water. The water turned into ink. Collectors who have seen these pens have come to believe that they were not manufactured solely for military use during the Ethiopian campaign: these pens are mostly a beautiful white, with a crest and the word "Etiopia" inscribed on the barrel. Such pens are occasionally found anywhere Aurora sold pens during the 1930s.

Although Parker promoted the Vacumatic pens from c.1932, it did not discontinue the Duofold button-filler until the aerometric-filler, which was designed to replace the Vacumatic range, was firmly established. The aerometric-filler was introduced on the 51 series in the 1950s. It had a semi-exposed sack, which was depressed simply by pressing a pressure bar, and as such it bore more than a passing resemblance to the old sleeve-filler system used briefly by Waterman during World War I.

Shortages of materials during World War II caused Waterman and Swan to abandon most of their complex technological "advances" of the 1930s, and both companies realized that the lever system or something similar was not such a bad idea after all, and the system continued in production until the 1950s. When Swan tried to make the pressure bar system more complicated in the 1950s by introducing a button at the end of the barrel to depress the pressure bar in a system similar to, but more complicated than, the old Parker Duofold button-filler of World War I vintage, the company went broke.

After the 1940s Waterman decided to go down-market, and the US company went out of business. It was rescued by its French subsidiary and soon adopted the French system of not having a filling system at all, but a removable cartridge made of transparent plastic in the barrel.

RIGHT **1937 Waterman Ink Vue demonstrator; 5 inches. The Ink Vue was Waterman's late 1930s attempt to make its pens more complicated, and thus more attractive from the technological point of view. Instead of the lever activating a pressure bar, which pressed directly on the sack, the lever splits in half and pumps a diaphragm inside a separate end section. This pumping action draws up a small amount of ink through a breather tube and into the** barrel. **The system is complicated to describe, to manufacture, and to use – for no noticeable benefit. The diaphragm system is similar in concept to Parker's Vacumatic system.**

LEFT **1935 "Etiopia" by Aurora; 4¾ inches. This pen was produced for use in the trenches by Italian officers in the Ethiopian campaign of 1936. Ink pellets are kept in a compartment in the blind cap at the end of the barrel. The pellets are inserted into the barrel, which is then filled with water to make ink.**

MODERN PENS

ABOVE **1917 trench safety pen by Moore; 5¼ inches. This pen carried a windowed container for ink pellets in the separate cap section. These were inserted into the barrel, which was then filled with water to make ink. It was designed for use by soldiers in the trenches who would not have had access to supplies of ink, and it was extensively advertised in the home markets as a suitable gift for a departing loved one.**

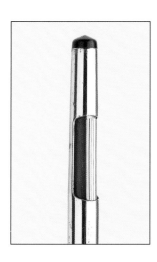

ABOVE **Parker aerometric filler.**

Today's manufacturers use one of two basic systems. The cartridge system is still widely used, and it is often found in conjunction with a refillable cylinder, usually similar to the old Waterman's sleeve-filler system. The other main principle is the suction-filler system, to which Montblanc and Pelikan have stayed relatively faithful since Pelikan developed it in the late 1920s. In this system, the end of the barrel is twisted to fill the pen, and this twisting draws back a simple suction-type plunger within the barrel. The plunger is usually held on the end of a telescopic tube in order to increase the ink supply.

Where did all the beautiful designs go? First, the Depression in the 1930s on both sides of the Atlantic made functionality and utilitarianism the order of the day. As in architecture, fashion in pen design dictated that the general impression created by the whole was more important than the minutiae of detail in the component parts.

Then, World War II and the consequent shortage of materials meant that even the top companies were forced to degrade their products in the light of what was available. Pens went further down-market, and became even more utilitarian than before. The poor quality of the war-time plastics is apparent from the way in which the pens have distorted with time and slight heat. The plastic barrels and caps can be seen to have shrunk around the internal metal components. Even when they were new it is likely that such pens were of poor quality. Contemporary reports indicate that people were advised that they would do better having a pre-war pen repaired than buying a new one.

Of equal importance in the decline in standards was the part played by commercialism. World pen marketing had always, by design or default, been American driven, and marketing principles came to play an ever more important role.

From the 1880s to the 1920s, pen manufacturers had emphasized quality and functionality, but now attention had shifted to the complexity of the mechanism. The

ABOVE **Mid-1930s Pelikan blue-lined model 100; 4½ inches. This twist-filler pen was the mainstay of the Pelikan line, surviving in substantially the same form from 1928 until it was finally phased out in the late 1940s.**

ABOVE **Late 1940s Waterman plastic presentation box; 7½ inches. At a period when Waterman was trying to go significantly down-market with such poor grade designs that** they eventually killed off the company, someone managed to design this presentation box, which must have outshone any fountain pen that the company could have produced to fill it.

LEFT **1940s lever-filler by Conway Stewart; 5¼ inches. Although attractive, the low-grade gold plating on this blue herringbone pen shows in the significant wear and pitting to the clip and lever.**

ABOVE & RIGHT **1940s Wahl-Eversharp Skyline set; 5¼ inches. This pen, with blue striation, was one of the better examples to appear during a difficult time for pen producers. Although some people find them attractive, it is clear that the manufacturer was having difficulties getting materials during World War II for this series of pens. Examples are often found with worn-out gold, shrunken, ill-** fitting parts, and the material has often become brittle and tends to crack unprovoked around the lever and barrel threads.

public, however, seemed uncertain whether this was a real advance, and manufacturers began to offer "lifetime guarantees" with their products. Soon pens without such guarantees could hardly be sold. As volumes increased, individuality was lost. Of even more fundamental interest to the companies producing pens was the necessity for making huge profits, often at the expense of all else. From this, a distinct lifecycle of pen companies has been discerned which militates heavily against continued production of objects of beauty.

The first part of the cycle involves setting up a company that competes with others by producing a product of high, hopefully higher, quality, and establishing a reputation based on that quality. This is followed by a period of increased pen production, during which the company produces pens in large numbers at slightly lesser quality. Thereafter there is a period when those running the company realize that they can maximise profits by trading on the reputation without necessarily following the tenets of quality at all. This period is then characterised by times of huge profits, which increase as the company moves relentlessly downhill in quality. In short, the quality of the pens deteriorates, but the marketing and the hype improves. Then suddenly, the management is taken by

surprise when the public realizes that the products are not what they expected, and the company finds itself without sales. Ultimately, the company goes bankrupt, and is forced into a take-over by one of their competitors, who themselves may still be at an earlier stage in the cycle, or by one of their overseas subsidiaries, who never believed the hype anyway. Backed by the banks, the new owners move the accountants in, and eventually someone realizes that they cannot revive the company without reviving the quality image at high sales levels.

LEFT 1940s lever-filler by Conway Stewart; 5¼ inches.

BELOW & BELOW RIGHT 1940s Montblanc no. 244; 5 inches. Similar to the pre-war Platinum Lined series, this post-war striped piston-filler set demonstrates that even during times of relative chaos, when the company was, in effect, being administered by Allied forces of occupation, Montblanc would not compromise on quality. This model, especially the striped version, is highly prized by collectors today, even though it did not carry the Meisterstück designation when it was produced.

ABOVE 1940 Parker no. 51; 5¼ inches. This pen, which survived in various forms for two decades, was one of the most popular pens produced by Parker. The number 51 marks the 51st anniversary of the company's foundation. Technologically advanced when it was introduced, it had a vacumatic-type filling system in which a diaphragm is repeatedly depressed, each time drawing a small amount of ink through a breather tube into the barrel. Later, Parker went over to an aerometric-type filler, which was similar to the sleeve-filler used 40 years before. Although it writes well for a pen that always had a rigid nib – apparently to speed the drying of the ink – the Parker no. 51 is not often of high value to the collector. Few models or colors are rare. Those that are worth looking out for include this example, with aluminum jewels at both ends (later ones used a pearl-type plastic jewel), and models with solid gold caps, including a two-tone example with the colored design resembling the shape of the Empire State Building in New York. Pre-production models were test-marketed in Venezuela before the pen's general introduction into the US, and these are very rare. They differ from the first-year models mainly in color.

COLLECTING FOUNTAIN PENS

CHAPTER 3

When you are offered or come across a fountain pen for sale, your first step should be to make sure that all parts are present, including the cap rings and end pieces. Check the wear on the gold-plating, which is difficult and expensive to repair, and look for any non-original parts, especially the nib. The inscription on the nib should generally match that on the barrel.

You may find yourself buying from a vendor who clearly knows little about pens. Look out for the use of words and phrases such as "lid" instead of "cap" and "continental" instead of "Italian safety," and for the description of a nib as "14 carat" – almost all nibs on valuable pens are 14 carat, and that will never be an important aspect of a pen that is offered for sale.

Always be wary, too, of vendors who say they have "just sold" or have a box full of pens they are unable to show you "at the moment." Such claims are more often than not worthless; the pens they say they have sold, especially if they say they are pens worth several thousand dollars, such as cupid or snake pens, almost certainly never existed.

WHAT TO COLLECT

The most desirable pens today are generally those made between 1900 and the mid-1930s. The qualities that make pens sought after are size, rarity, workmanship, including the complexity of the artwork, and the presence of precious stones in the design. Pens with filigree work over hard rubber are more valuable than pens without such work, and pens with pierced and engraved work tend to be more valuable than those decorated with filigree work.

LEFT **1905 Waterman no. 418; 5⅝ inches. This fine silver filigree pen is an eyedropper model. From c. 1902, floral motifs began to appear in the filigree patterns. The design** shown here is one of the earlier patterns, but they were changed frequently. Most of the fine silver designs had the same filigree pattern on the barrel.

SIZE Considerations of size are relatively self-explanatory. In collecting terms, the most desirable pens are the Waterman (or Swan) no. 20; the Parker Giant, both black and red; the Montblanc no. 12 safety pen; and the Namiki Giant. Although it is not quite as large, the LeBoeuf no. 75 or no. 90 is also desirable, principally because the plastics used are so beautiful. Ladies' pens do not command the same values as their larger counterparts. All the large pens have an inescapable aura about them that is sometimes divorced from their actual beauty.

ABOVE **Early 1910s Waterman no. 420. The largest, most desirable, and rarest of the standard production filigree pens, this eyedropper-filler is known in only about four examples worldwide.**

BELOW **1910 Waterman no. 218; 5⅜ inches. This sterling silver pen is half-covered with an overlay of an etched floral pattern.**

LEFT **1930 watch pen; manufacturer Swiss, but unknown; senior size. This high quality, craftsman-produced twist-filler has a watch mounted in the crown. It is marked "CB" on the cap and "Bucherer" on the dial. Bucherer was the original retailer, and although the company is still in existence, it does not keep records of the items bought or the manufacturers with which it did business.**

BELOW **1905 safety pen by Moore in ultra-large jumbo size; 6¼ inches.**

ABOVE **1920s giant eyedropper by Dunhill-Namiki; 6¼ inches. The design is of a horseman in front of a mountain with trees.**

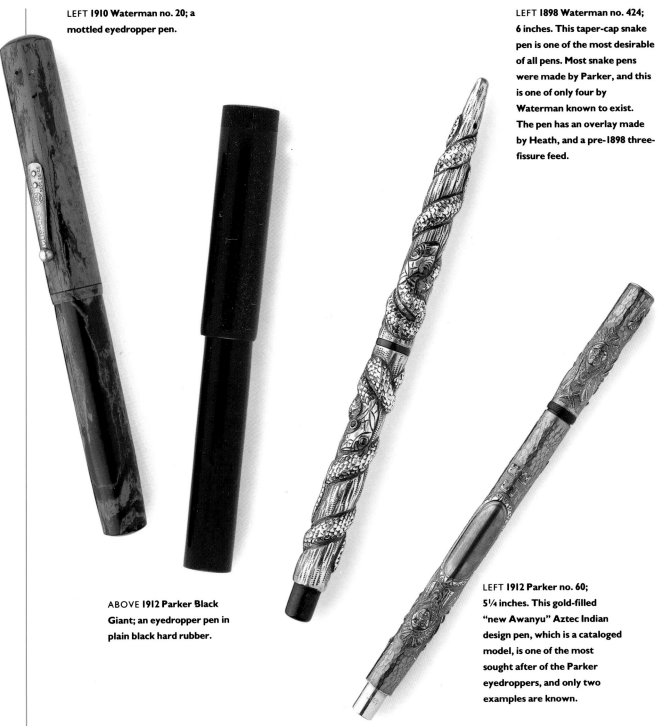

LEFT **1910 Waterman no. 20; a mottled eyedropper pen.**

LEFT **1898 Waterman no. 424; 6 inches. This taper-cap snake pen is one of the most desirable of all pens. Most snake pens were made by Parker, and this is one of only four by Waterman known to exist. The pen has an overlay made by Heath, and a pre-1898 three-fissure feed.**

ABOVE **1912 Parker Black Giant; an eyedropper pen in plain black hard rubber.**

LEFT **1912 Parker no. 60; 5¼ inches. This gold-filled "new Awanyu" Aztec Indian design pen, which is a cataloged model, is one of the most sought after of the Parker eyedroppers, and only two examples are known.**

WORKMANSHIP Although the concept of beauty in complexity is a fact that seems to have been forgotten at the time of the Depression, some of the earlier pens were works of art in themselves. Pens decorated with intricately handcarved snakes, Aztec heads, tree-trunk designs, or cupids always form the centerpiece of any collection. The rarer pens decorated with the elegant piercing and engraving work that was carried out in intricate detail are, in general, exceptionally desirable. Also sought after are pens decorated with Japanese handpainting known as maki'e work. Although all these decorated pens are keenly collected, even more desirable are pens that combine handengraved motifs with elegant piercing and engraving work – such as the cupid-decorated safety pens, usually made by Waterman.

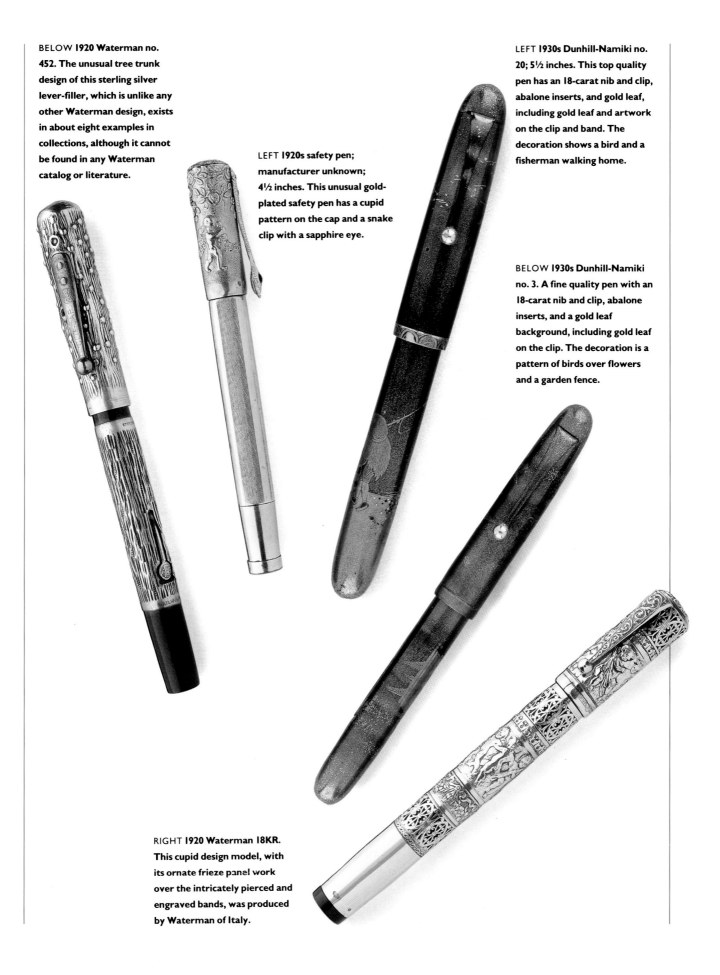

BELOW **1920 Waterman no. 452. The unusual tree trunk design of this sterling silver lever-filler, which is unlike any other Waterman design, exists in about eight examples in collections, although it cannot be found in any Waterman catalog or literature.**

LEFT **1920s safety pen; manufacturer unknown; 4½ inches. This unusual gold-plated safety pen has a cupid pattern on the cap and a snake clip with a sapphire eye.**

LEFT **1930s Dunhill-Namiki no. 20; 5½ inches. This top quality pen has an 18-carat nib and clip, abalone inserts, and gold leaf, including gold leaf and artwork on the clip and band. The decoration shows a bird and a fisherman walking home.**

BELOW **1930s Dunhill-Namiki no. 3. A fine quality pen with an 18-carat nib and clip, abalone inserts, and a gold leaf background, including gold leaf on the clip. The decoration is a pattern of birds over flowers and a garden fence.**

RIGHT **1920 Waterman 18KR. This cupid design model, with its ornate frieze panel work over the intricately pierced and engraved bands, was produced by Waterman of Italy.**

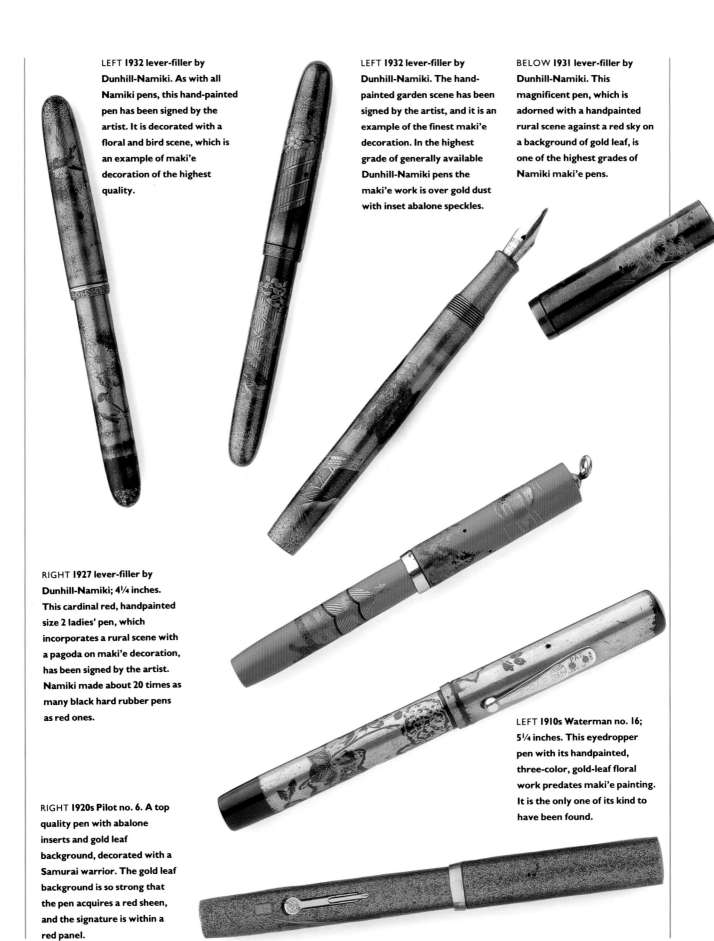

LEFT **1932 lever-filler by Dunhill-Namiki. As with all Namiki pens, this hand-painted pen has been signed by the artist. It is decorated with a floral and bird scene, which is an example of maki'e decoration of the highest quality.**

LEFT **1932 lever-filler by Dunhill-Namiki. The hand-painted garden scene has been signed by the artist, and it is an example of the finest maki'e decoration. In the highest grade of generally available Dunhill-Namiki pens the maki'e work is over gold dust with inset abalone speckles.**

BELOW **1931 lever-filler by Dunhill-Namiki. This magnificent pen, which is adorned with a handpainted rural scene against a red sky on a background of gold leaf, is one of the highest grades of Namiki maki'e pens.**

RIGHT **1927 lever-filler by Dunhill-Namiki; 4¼ inches. This cardinal red, handpainted size 2 ladies' pen, which incorporates a rural scene with a pagoda on maki'e decoration, has been signed by the artist. Namiki made about 20 times as many black hard rubber pens as red ones.**

LEFT **1910s Waterman no. 16; 5¼ inches. This eyedropper pen with its handpainted, three-color, gold-leaf floral work predates maki'e painting. It is the only one of its kind to have been found.**

RIGHT **1920s Pilot no. 6. A top quality pen with abalone inserts and gold leaf background, decorated with a Samurai warrior. The gold leaf background is so strong that the pen acquires a red sheen, and the signature is within a red panel.**

However rare these pens were, they did feature in catalogs and could be ordered through ordinary dealers. Rarer still are the pens that did not feature in catalogs at all, principally because of the complex workmanship. Pens decorated with precious stones fall into this category, because they were normally ordered only as special presentation pieces. Even less often encountered are the individually signed pens, such as the Waterman safety pen featuring Jesus Christ, or pens decorated with scenes from classical literature. These pens were usually made or commissioned by Waterman of Italy. Although fakes abound and were of particular concern to Waterman at the time, the manufacture of such pens only harmed the companies' profits and, as long as they are well made, these pens are almost as valuable as those made by the major companies they sought to emulate.

BELOW **1937 Eversharp Coronet; 5 inches.** This gold-plated, lever-filler pen was one of the most beautiful pens to be produced during the 1930s, and it features inserts in either black or burgundy colored Pyralin. A solid gold model was produced with diamonds set in the Pyralin which was presented to heads of state. None has appeared on the market.

ABOVE **1900 eyedropper pen by A. A. Waterman; 5⅛ inches.** The silver art nouveau filigree is further decorated with inset miner-cut diamonds.

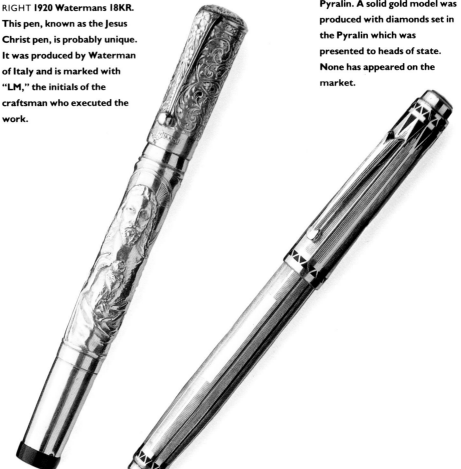

RIGHT **1920 Watermans 18KR.** This pen, known as the Jesus Christ pen, is probably unique. It was produced by Waterman of Italy and is marked with "**LM**," the initials of the craftsman who executed the work.

Perhaps rarest of all are the pens that one hears about but will probably never see. In this category are the few items described in the Fabergé order books, which were elegantly mounted over Onoto mechanicals for Russian princes *c.*1912; and the fabled Eversharp Coronets, which were made in the late 1930s of solid gold and studded with diamonds around the crown. Such pens were made for presentation to heads of state, and it is unlikely that many will find their way onto the market.

BELOW **1910s Waterman no. 214; 5½ inches. This pen, with its repoussé rose pattern in sterling silver, is an exceptionally rare and desirable example of a half-covered design.**

LEFT *c.*1914 **Parker no. 15. The barrel is of alternating abalone and mother-of-pearl mounted on red hard rubber, and the cap is filigree. Red overlays appeared late in the production cycle of the no. 15, and they are exceptionally rare.**

BELOW **1920 Montblanc no. 00; 3¼ inches. This safety pen, with its exceptionally rare spider design filigree work, has been much copied recently.**

RIGHT **1900s Waterman no. 404. The heavy lily repoussé design is in sterling silver. Only one example is known to exist in a private collection.**

LEFT **1910 piston-filler by Onoto; 4½ inches. The art nouveau design is enameled over the sterling silver "filigree-effect."**

LEFT **1915 crescent-filler by Conklin; 5¼ inches. This engine-turned, 14-carat gold pen is the only solid gold crescent-filler in a private collection.**

RIGHT **1900s Parker no. 11; 5½ inches. Parker produced these aluminum barreled, taper-cap, eyedropper pens during the first decades of the 20th century, but few have survived. This one has the design cut into the aluminum, which is black-anodized. Aluminum was considered a precious metal in the early 1900s.**

LEFT **1902 eyedropper pen by Paul E. Wirt; 5½ inches. This taper-cap pen has a curlicue design in sterling silver filigree. In the last decade of the 19th century, Wirt was the largest manufacturer of fountain pens, producing more than almost all other companies combined. The company's patents date back to 1873.**

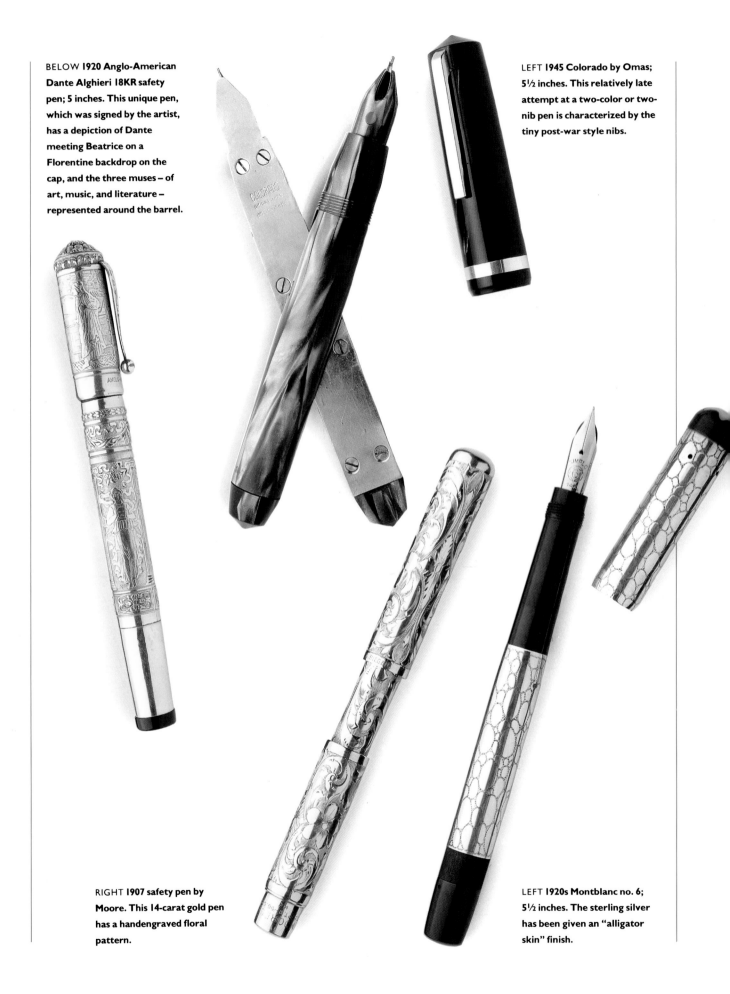

BELOW **1920 Anglo-American Dante Alghieri 18KR safety pen; 5 inches.** This unique pen, which was signed by the artist, has a depiction of Dante meeting Beatrice on a Florentine backdrop on the cap, and the three muses – of art, music, and literature – represented around the barrel.

LEFT **1945 Colorado by Omas; 5½ inches.** This relatively late attempt at a two-color or two-nib pen is characterized by the tiny post-war style nibs.

RIGHT **1907 safety pen by Moore.** This 14-carat gold pen has a handengraved floral pattern.

LEFT **1920s Montblanc no. 6; 5½ inches.** The sterling silver has been given an "alligator skin" finish.

FILIGREE PENS Filigree pens were made from *c.*1897 onwards by most companies. The early examples, often Waterman, were made of fine silver and were marked "Fine Silver 999°/oo1000." The metal was generally so soft that the pens did not wear well. The original designs were whirling lines in no particular form. After a few years the patterns tended to be based on floral motifs, and curlicues were also found on the early pens, although these are very rare. After *c.*1903 the designs tended to become standardized around patterns resembling either paisley or leaf designs and, later, sheaves of bamboo. Designs other than by Waterman – by Parker and Conklin, for example – tended to have patterns based on either a three- or four-leaf motif.

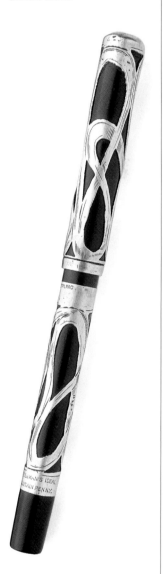

BELOW **1898 Waterman no. 412. This eyedropper pen is decorated with fine silver filigree. The earliest designs featured long, flowing lines or occasionally short curlicues on the fine silver.**

ABOVE **1900 safety pen by Moore; 5⅝ inches. The earlier pens by Moore had a short cap that, like Moore's later style as well as Waterman's caps, was designed to fit onto the end of the barrel. Although the gold-filled filigree is not quite as fine as the filigree on Waterman or Parker pens, it is exceptionally beautiful.**

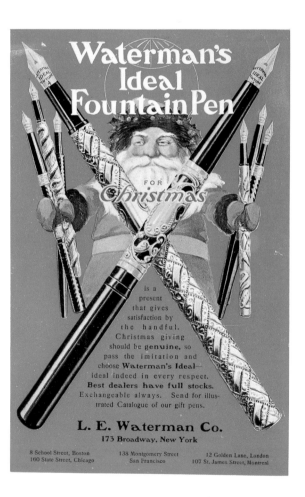

ABOVE **A 1910 advertisement for Waterman pens.**

Rare pens by Sheaffer are decorated with beautiful, highly stylized art nouveau swirls.

Filigree pens started to peter out towards the end of the 1920s, when mass-production techniques made it no longer cost-effective to produce them. The overlay had to be put in position by hand and the metalwork had to be carefully heated, procedures that did not lend themselves to mass-production. Therefore, although filigree pens were made in the 1930s – Waterman's Night and Day pattern in sizes 452 and 454, or a fine pattern resembling rabbit ears or marihuana leaves, usually found in size 494, for example – they are relatively rare.

BELOW **1906 Waterman; 5½ inches. As well as being cardinal red, this model was made in fine silver, which was** relatively unusual because the silver did not wear well. Note the graceful art nouveau long, swirling lines to the design.

RIGHT **1905 Waterman. Fine silver filigree over black. As well as being cardinal black, this model was made in fine silver. This was relatively unusual because the silver did** not wear well. Note the graceful art nouveau long, swirling lines to the design.

ABOVE **1902 eyedropper pen by Carey; 6 inches. This exceptionally rare, middle-joint pen has fine silver filigree work overlaid on red and black mottled hard rubber. Filigree** work over anything but black is very rare and desirable. This pen has a Van Valkenburgh clip. This was the first clip designed to be attached to the pen cap, and until they designed their own, most major pen companies in the US used the Van Valkenburgh clip.

RIGHT **1910 safety pen by Moore in gold-filled filigree; 4½ inches.**

LEFT **1906 crescent-filler by Conklin; ladies' size. The decoration is gold-filled art nouveau filigree.**

RIGHT **1908 twist-filler by A. A. Waterman. The photograph of this gold-filled filigree pen shows that Heath was not the only company executing filigree work for a number of pen companies.**

LEFT **1900 Aikin Lambert. The sterling silver art nouveau filigree is another unusual use of repoussé work on the metal filigree, this time made rarer by having a seldom seen ribbon scroll design.**

RIGHT **1915 Parker no. 14; 4½ inches. A sterling silver button-filler.**

LEFT **1900 eyedropper pen by A. A. Waterman; 5¼ inches. With gold-filled art nouveau filigree pattern.**

RIGHT **1908 Parker no. 16 Jack-Knife safety. A gold-filled filigree, eyedropper baby pen.**

RIGHT **1912 Waterman no. 12v. Although it is tiny, this sterling silver filigree checkbook pen had a size 2 nib, as did most small US Waterman models. The bulging cap crown was designed to fit into the spine of a checkbook.**

LEFT *c.* **1908 Waterman no. 514. This 14-carat eyedropper pen has a repoussé (chased) filigree design. A few examples of this type of pen have been found, although Waterman's catalogs of the time do not describe it. It does, however, feature in the company's advertisements.**

The most desirable of the filigree pens are the exceptionally rare Montblanc examples in spider, electric ray, or an art deco pattern, and the Waterman or Parker designs, which were mounted over hard red rubber.

Unfortunately, fakes abound. In addition, when the pens were originally sold, it was not uncommon to have jewelers mount filigree work on the pens when they were ordered, and sometimes, too, the manufacturers would either send out pens for decoration or buy in work from specialized filigree manufacturers; in the US this was often a company called Heath.

It is important to check any filigree pen carefully to establish whether it started life with this decoration. The number of a Waterman pen made in North America should reflect every element of the company's numbering system: if filigree work has been mounted over an ordinary red pen, the number will be 52, indicating that the pen was not originally decorated with filigree. On the other hand, most UK Waterman size 2 pens tend to have 52 on the base whatever the material, and all Italian Waterman rolled gold safety pens have 42 or 44 on the barrel end and "18KR" on the metalwork.

Also check that there is no chasing, engine turning, or inscription of any kind under the filigree. Pen companies would have had no reason to mount filigree work on an already finished pen, and the last stage in the manufacture of a non-filigree pen was the insertion of the inscription on the barrel.

ADVICE WHEN BUYING PENS

The following list is intended to assist in negotiation when buying fountain pens, and to put you in a position of knowing as much as, or more about the pen you are trying to buy, than the vendor. In many cases repairs are possible and hence should not affect the price but many repairs are difficult and in such cases you should negotiate the price down.

TROUBLE SHOOTER

The sack is hard and dry	Sacks are almost always replaceable.
The piston is dry and will not move or suck up ink	If the piston is of cork, find a cork washer; if it is a ring (as in a Sheaffer), it can be replaced; if it is a washer (as in an Onoto), it will be difficult to find a replacement.
The plunger is dry and will not move or suck up ink	Montblanc and Pelikan plungers can be renewed, but Conklin Nozak plungers are difficult to replace.
The cap lip is cracked	If the material is not too rare this can be repaired (at a high cost), although putting the cap on the barrel end just once may break a glued split.
The cap itself is cracked	This is difficult to repair.
The barrel threads are cracked	This is difficult to repair, expensive, and requires professional help. The threads may be carried farther up the barrel and the whole pen shortened, or new threads may be machined on.
The lever is broken	A replacement is usually necessary, and will be moderately expensive.
The clip is broken	Replacement clips can often be found.
The clip has sprung away from the cap	It can be bent back if it has not split.
There is a burn mark on the pen	Holes can occasionally be filled. Price should be negotiated down substantially.
The plastic is crazed	The ends of Waterman's Hundred Year Pens can be replaced, but the problem is usually terminal with LeBoeufs and Eversharp Dorics.
The cap will not screw on	Check the threads for cracks, but wear is usually the cause. Threads can sometimes be built up or the barrel threads expanded to give a better fit.
The nib is split or the iridium has broken off	Splits can be welded together and new iridium can be welded on, although this is specialized work that should be undertaken by professionals. The repaired nib may still be prone to splitting.
The nib is bent	Nibs can be straightened.
The barrel is distorted, especially around the lever	This is most likely on fairly cheap pens. The problem is not curable.
The plastic is discolored	This is unlikely to be ink staining, although it is worth checking. There is no known repair.
Black hard rubber has turned brown	The rubber can be polished and cleaned.
The nib will not come out of a safety pen	It is often merely jammed, but be extremely careful not to break the spiral while you are releasing it.
The nib on a safety pen flops in and out	The spiral is broken. It is unlikely that this can be repaired permanently, and replacements are difficult to find unless, of course, it is a common make.
The filigree is broken	This is usually irreparable. It is rarely possible to take off filigree from a spare pen to replace another one.
An abalone panel is cracked	The whole panel may be replaceable, or the crack may be minimized if it is removed and cleaned.

FOUNTAIN PEN MANUFACTURERS

CHAPTER 4

The following companies produced pens that are now sought after by collectors throughout the world. Prices may easily run into several thousand dollars.

AURORA 1919 to the present; an Italian company. This company started producing pens in hard rubber in the early 1920s, and was using Celluloid by 1925. It's designs were based on the Duofold styles and colors and the pens often had filigree cap crowns. Aurora also made elegant safety pens in rolled gold. During the 1930s, it developed a clip with a locking mechanism that had to be disengaged before the pen could be removed from the pocket. The pens had button fillers or lever fillers. After 1940 production was standardized around the model 88, which was designed to resemble the Parker 51.

LEFT **1906 crescent-filler by Conklin. A ladies' pen with gold-filled, art nouveau filigree.**

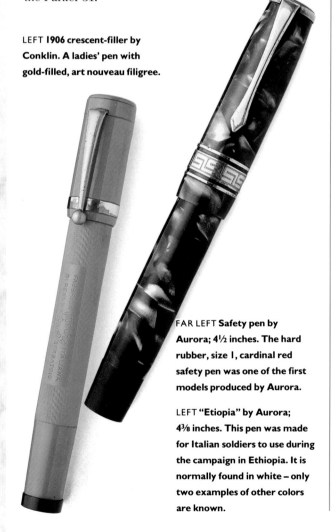

FAR LEFT **Safety pen by Aurora; 4½ inches. The hard rubber, size 1, cardinal red safety pen was one of the first models produced by Aurora.**

LEFT **"Etiopia" by Aurora; 4⅜ inches. This pen was made for Italian soldiers to use during the campaign in Ethiopia. It is normally found in white – only two examples of other colors are known.**

CONKLIN 1898–1940s; a US company. Nib sizes ranged from 2 to 8, although there was little uniformity. The company introduced the first practical self-filling mechanism in the US – a crescent-shaped pressure bar protruded from the barrel and was held in place by a locking ring – but it was overtaken by Sheaffer's development in the early to mid-1910s of the lever-filler, which obviated the need for a protruding crescent, and by Parker's development of the pocket clip. Like Parker, it toyed with green woodgrain hard rubber c.1903. In the late 1910s it became a smallish, regional US manufacturer and went over to the production of lever-fillers with its square-shaped Endura range. It followed this with the Nozak and Symmetrik plunge-fillers in the 1930s. Early filigree overlay pens are often elaborate – and are very rare and valuable. Plastic pens made after the mid-1920s are of medium value and are rarely found outside the US. Pens produced after 1940 have no value whatsoever, the quality of the company's products declining more sharply than those of almost any other company.

THOMAS DE LA RUE 1881–1957; a UK company, whose pens were known as Onoto or Pelican. Nib sizes ranged from 2 to 8. The company introduced stylographic pens, and then marketed a mid-jointed type of eyedropper model (the Pelican) until its collaboration with a transvestite, roller-skating vaudeville artiste-cum-inventor, George Sweetser, who invented the piston-filling technique at the turn of the century. The company continued to produce piston-filling models until it went out of business, although it did produce lever-fillers during the 1930s. The pens made before the 1920s are very valuable if they are elaborate, especially if they are metal or silver enamel models.

DUNN 1921–24; a US company. This company's fame lies solely in its production of two piston-filling pens – the Super Dreadnought and the Super Giant – which are so huge that they dwarf almost all other pens. Apart from these two pens, the company's pens are of only average quality and made of average quality hard rubber or transparent Bakelite, to which time has definitely not been kind. The nibs, most of which have split in numerous places since they were made, were made of particularly thin gold.

FENDOGRAPH Nothing is known about this company, which may have been German, except that it produced some exceptionally beautiful rolled gold safety pens or button-fillers, often with enameled decoration. It may have had some connection with the significantly inferior company Fend.

KAWECO 1892–1970; a German company. Many different models of silver and gold-plated pens, often inlaid with precious stones, were made between 1900 and 1925. The pens were usually safety models with threads on the barrel end for screwing into special cap threads, but the company also produced many other filling systems using both pistons and sacks.

RIGHT *c.1920* safety pen by Kaweco; 5 inches. This gold-filled pen has diamonds and rubies inset in a floral pattern on the cap.

ABOVE **Dia 25 by Kaweco.**

LEBOEUF 1918–36; a US company. Nib sizes ranged from 2 to 8. The company patented a method for making barrels and caps out of tubing rather than having to drill them out of rod. It was thus able to use different, usually more beautiful, materials than its competitors. It also used a barrel liner made of metal and claimed that its pens were, therefore, unbreakable. All its models were lever-fillers until *c*.1930; thereafter it used the barrel to operate as a full or half-length sleeve-filler. The company may have moved from Springfield, Massachusetts, to West Springfield during the Depression after stock scandals led to its being taken over by a member of the family called Eugene LeBoeuf. The company latterly made holy water sprinklers.

MABIE, TODD 1860s–1958; an Anglo-American company, known also as Swan and, before 1908, as Mabie, Todd & Bard. Nib sizes ranged from 1 to 10, although there is no uniformity in the larger sizes. This major worldwide manufacturer originated in the US, but operated almost exclusively from the UK after the early 1900s, even making high quality pens for a few years after World War II. Cheaper pens sold as Blackbird, Swallow, and Jackdaw. The company's pens are usually eyedropper models, lever-fillers, or simple twist-fillers, in which the knob at the end of the barrel connects directly with a paddle inside the barrel, which, in turn, depresses the sack. It continued the production of eyedropper pens well into the 1950s for export to countries where high temperatures caused the rapid deterioration of the rubber in the sack. There is no connection with the Japanese company of the same name.

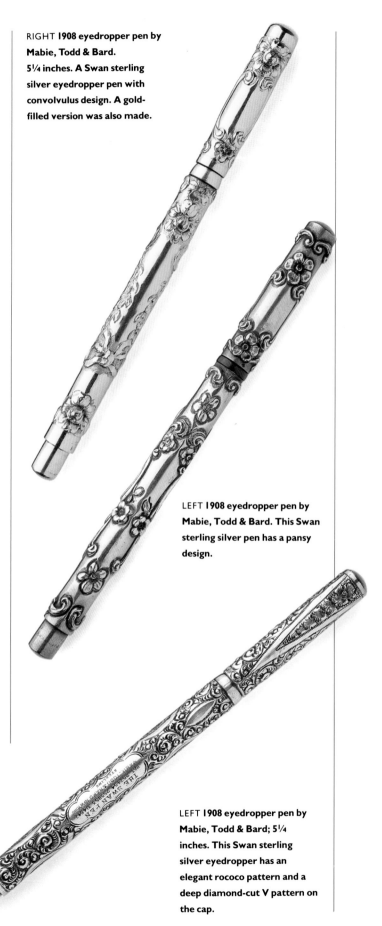

RIGHT **1908 eyedropper pen by Mabie, Todd & Bard. 5¼ inches. A Swan sterling silver eyedropper pen with convolvulus design. A gold-filled version was also made.**

LEFT **1908 eyedropper pen by Mabie, Todd & Bard. This Swan sterling silver pen has a pansy design.**

LEFT **1908 eyedropper pen by Mabie, Todd & Bard; 5¼ inches. This Swan sterling silver eyedropper has an elegant rococo pattern and a deep diamond-cut V pattern on the cap.**

BELOW 1934 Montblanc no. 124; 4½ inches. A Meisterstück 14 carat engine-turned, push-knob filler. During the late 1920s Montblanc used a button-type filler, which was activated by unscrewing the blind cap at the end of the barrel. This did not come off the pen, but was merely pushed to activate the pressure bar. It was an improvement over the ordinary button filler because the blind cap did not come off and could not, therefore, be mislaid.

MONTBLANC 1910 to the present; a German company, known originally as Simplo Filler Pen Co. or Rouge et Noir. Nib sizes range from 00 to 12, although after 1926 top-level pens, known as Masterpiece, Meisterstück, Chef d'Oeuvre, or Capolavoro (which were originally offered as "lifetime guarantee" pens to boost sales), had only 4810 on the nib. The company used the number 4810 because Mont Blanc, after which the company was named, is 15,700 feet high. Look out for safety pens made in the 1910s, 1920s, and 1930s; for twist-button fillers made in the late 1920s and early 1930s; and for piston-fillers made in the late 1930s. All Montblanc pens are valuable, even those made after World War II but before 1962, especially if they are colored or metal. There was significant, although largely undocumented production of unusual or valuable pens, including elaborate 18-carat safety pens, outside Germany in, for example, Denmark, Spain and Italy, and, apparently, also in South America. During the mid-1920s, the company experimented with other filling mechanisms such as blow-fillers, although most models of this kind were sold in France, and pump, and idiosyncratic lever-fillers. Production for the German market concentrated on black models.

RIGHT 1920 Montblanc no. 2; 4½ inches. This safetypen, which is signed by the artist, "Meazza," has a repoussé art nouveau, gold-filled barrel and cap. The pen was produced for Montblanc of Italy by a local craftsman, and is signed Montblanc on the cap.

BELOW 1920 Montblanc no. 4; 5½ inches. Montblanc pens with lever-filling systems are extremely rare, especially with sterling silver filigree work of this caliber.

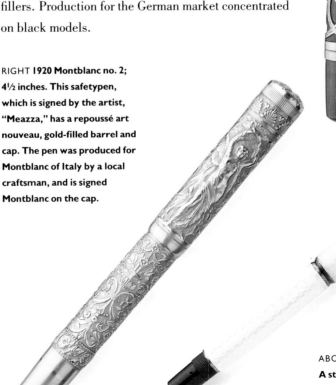

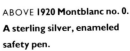

ABOVE 1920 Montblanc no. 0. A sterling silver, enameled safety pen.

MOORE 1898–1950s; a US company, sometimes referred to as the Boston Fountain Pen Co. Usually no size is visible on the nib, although originally the nibs bore the words "American Fountain Pen Company." The number on the pen often refers to the price. The company produced valuable safety pens in metal or in elaborate filigree patterns until the mid-1910s. Thereafter, it became a small, Boston-based, regional producer, making very low value pens in poor quality hard rubber and, later, completely undistinguished pens in plastic. In the 1950s it tried to make a comeback with the Fingerpoint pen, which purported to copy the success of both the Sheaffer Snorkel and the Parker 51. The effort finished off the company altogether.

NAMIKI 1924 to the present; a Japanese company, now known as Pilot. Nib sizes are 1–6, 20 and 50. The company copied western models and made pen-related products until 1924, when it developed and patented lacquering techniques for handpainted decoration (maki'e) that did not discolor or fade. It exported pens worldwide until 1930, when it signed a marketing agreement with Alfred Dunhill of London. Thereafter and until 1940 it was known in all countries in which Dunhill marketed products as Dunhill-Namiki. All the company's pens are valuable. Quality ranges from the lowest (with a lacquered, solid gold band) to the highest (with maki'e work on all plastic and metal parts on a background of gold dust with inset speckles of abalone). The company also made top quality pens with the artist's signature on a red shield and lacquering over and around silver filigree work.

RIGHT **1902 safety pen by Moore. A slender model with repoussé sterling silver covering and an early short cap.**

LEFT **1915 improved safety pen by Moore; 5⅖ inches. Not to be confused with a sleeve-filler, this pen is a push-type safety retractor pen.**

RIGHT **1936 eyedropper pen by Dunhill-Namiki. This handpainted example, which was signed by the artist, is "new old stock." The size 3 pen has a traditional ink-flow valve at the end of the barrel and bird of paradise decoration.**

LEFT **1939 eyedropper pen by Pilot. This handpainted pen, decorated with a Maki'e Japanese lady, was signed by the artist. It is a very late example, and uses the clip with which Pilot standardized its high quality products after World War II.**

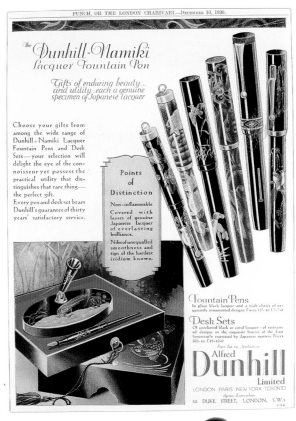

The Dunhill-Namiki
Lacquer Fountain Pen

Gifts of enduring beauty...
and utility...each a genuine
specimen of Japanese lacquer

Choose your gifts from
among the wide range of
Dunhill-Namiki Lacquer
Fountain Pens and Desk
Sets—your selection will
delight the eye of the con-
noisseur yet possess the
practical utility that dis-
tinguishes that rare thing—
the perfect gift.
Every pen and desk set bears
Dunhill's guarantee of thirty
years' satisfactory service.

Points
of
Distinction

Non-inflammable

Covered with
layers of genuine
Japanese lacquer
of everlasting
brilliance.

Nibs of unequalled
smoothness and
tips of the hardest
iridium known.

Fountain Pens
In plain black lacquer and a wide choice of ex-
quisitely ornamented designs. Prices 18/- to £7-7-0

Desk Sets
Of unrelieved black or coral lacquer—of restrain-
ed designs or the exquisite fancies of the East
luxuriously expressed by Japanese masters. Prices
30/- to £10-10-0

Price list on Application

Alfred
Dunhill
Limited

LONDON PARIS NEW YORK TORONTO
Agents Everywhere
30 DUKE STREET, LONDON, S.W.1

OMAS 1919 to the present; also known as Zerolo. The company originally produced pens with built-in thermometers for doctors, and arrow-clip examples together with very valuable Bayer Celluloid or Platinum Lined (PL) Extra Lucens pens. Zerolo pens are keenly collected; they have two separate nibs spiraling out of the barrel in the manner of a safety pen, but with two integral containers for the sacks. These were matchstick-fillers, and were called Unic in France and John Dunhill in the UK. A rarer Zerolo model has a short, separate pen assembly inserted into the upper half of the barrel. Rarer still is the Zerolo pen, known as Itala, which has alternate nib assemblies, shooting out of the barrel when a blind cap is pulled. The company produced Europa pens for the World's Fair held in Italy in 1936. It also manufactured sub-brands and parts for other companies and pen assemblers, whose products can, therefore, closely resemble Omas pens.

ABOVE **An early 1930s advertisement for Dunhill-Namiki products.**

RIGHT **1930 Extra by Omas; 5 inches.**

LEFT **1936 eyedropper pen by Dunhill-Namiki; 5¼ inches. This handpainted size 3 pen was signed by the artist. It is "new old stock," and has the traditional ink-flow valve at the end of the barrel and decoration.**

LEFT **1936 Lucens by Omas; junior size; 4 inches.**

PARKER 1891 to the present; a US company, UK-owned for a while after the 1970s, but now (1993) US-owned once more. Early pens (up to 1920) are sometimes elaborate, although almost never in solid gold, and are very valuable, with nib sizes from 2 to 12. The company's numbering system is impenetrable: it may be chronological, but most models tended to remain in production until the introduction of the Duofold range in the early 1920s; including, at first, a filthy model called the jointless, which was filled by grasping the nib and feed with the fingers and pulling them out manually. All red, mottled or green woodgrain eyedropper pens, filigree pens, and metal pens are valuable, and few were made after the introduction of the Duofold range. Most subsequent pens were mass-produced. The company went in for large-scale, mass-production after the Depression, leading to the production of the Vacumatic, and few valuable pens were made until the 1970s, when there was limited production of sea-floor metal and rare wood pens.

RIGHT *c.*1912 Parker no. 46; 5½ inches. This eyedropper pen has a mother-of-pearl fluted barrel. Of the taper-cap pens, the rarest designs are the gold-filled taper caps, whether repoussé or filigree.

BELOW 1915 Parker no. 14; 4½ inches. A sterling silver button-filler.

RIGHT *c.*1912 Parker no. 15. This ladies' pen has a mother-of-pearl barrel over black hard rubber and a filigree turban cap.

LEFT Mid-1940s Parker no. 51; 5½ inches. This model has a gold-filled cap. Note the hooded nib, which was revolutionary when it was first introduced.

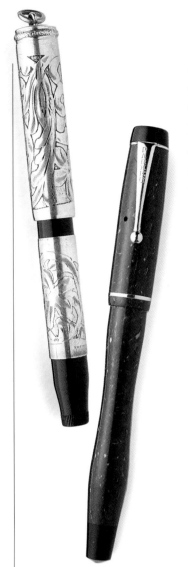

ARTHUR A. WATERMAN & CO. 1895–*c*.1920; a US company, originally called the Modern Fountain Pen Co. The company's numbering system is unfathomable. It commenced business making a middle-joint eyedropper system to prevent ink leaking onto the fingers. It then tried to compete with the L. E. Waterman Co. by using the Waterman name and by having a similar range of high quality, metal-overlaid pens based on a twist-filling system and using, curiously, a rubber sack that was open at both ends. Early metal-overlaid pens are very elaborate and valuable. In 1902, however, it fell foul of the other company, and was forced to mark all its pens with the disclaimer "A. A. Waterman Modern Pen Company, not related to the L. E. Waterman Company." The lawsuit seems to have brought on financial difficulties, and the company quickly went downhill. Later pens are indistinguishable from low caliber Good Service Pen Company models, and production petered out in the 1920s.

BELOW **1905 twist-filler by A. A. Waterman. This art nouveau patterned twist-filler has a heavy repoussé rococo floral design on the gold-filled cap and barrel. This was a very early attempt at producing a self-filler. A tubular sack was fixed to the section at one end and to the turning-piece at the other. The twisting movement expelled air from the sack, which inflated in the ink when it was unwound.**

ABOVE LEFT **1920 Parker no. 32 Lucky Curve; 4½ inches. This sterling silver pen, with an acid-etched floral pattern, is a full-size ladies' or vest pocket (ring-top) pen. Until the early 1920s it was fashionable to wear vest-pocket pens on a cord or chain, and it is often difficult to differentiate between vest-pocket pens and ladies' pens.**

ABOVE RIGHT **Late 1920s Parker Duofold. This lapis blue pen is the ultra-rare Zaner Blouser model. This peculiarly shaped pen was produced by the factory for the Zaner Blouser calligraphy school, and it was made to the school's design to facilitate drawing and calligraphy. Few examples have survived.**

RIGHT **1905 twister-filler by A. A. Waterman; 6 inches. Note the art nouveau pattern resembling repoussé sea shells.**

LEFT **1912 Waterman no. 0524;** 5½ inches. The pattern of this gold-filled repoussé eyedropper pen with gold-filled repoussé taper cap is known as the pineapple design. Only two examples of this model are known.

ABOVE **1905 Waterman no. 0324; 5½ inches. The patch** design, half-covered, gold-filled eyedropper pen has a taper cap.

RIGHT **1920s safety pen; possibly by Waterman; 5 inches. The pen is marked 18KR, meaning 18 carat rolled gold, and it has a Greek key pattern on the cap and a classical romantic scene around the barrel.**

BELOW **1910 Waterman no. 418; 5⅜ inches. A cardinal red pen with sterling silver filigree. Exceptionally unusual with the size 8 nib, this was the more often seen style of filigree, which was used from c.1903 until 1920.**

LEFT **1900 Waterman repoussé sterling silver multi-floral** pattern eyedropper. Although most manufacturers used repoussé techniques in making their pens, this was the only one that Waterman appeared to make.

RIGHT **1912 Waterman no. 12v. Although this cardinal red checkbook pen is tiny, it has a size 2 nib, as did most US Waterman pens. The bulging cap crown was designed to fit into the spine of a checkbook.**

L. E. WATERMAN & CO. 1882 to the present; a US company, which was French-owned only after the 1940s. Nib sizes range from 1 to 10. Eyedropper pens made from 1882 to 1915, and any early unusual filling systems, are very valuable, especially in the United States. All larger size filigree pens are keenly collected, as are any model of the 1930s Patrician series, although the similar but smaller Lady Patricia series is less collectable. The company developed the mottled hard rubber finish into the woodgrain and, ultimately, the ripple finish. UK pens are marked "F.D.W."; French pens are marked "Jif-Waterman." Pens made after *c.*1941 decrease dramatically in value.

WHITWORTH 1910–15; a UK company. These pens, made by the City Pen Manufacturing Company, were very large, often sterling silver safety pens. In the mid-1910s the company linked up with Valentine, which was later taken over by Parker when that company wanted to launch its products in the UK. The name is often also found spelled as Whytwarth.

MEDIUM-VALUE PENS

Given the constraints of being unable to find quality materials in war-time or otherwise going downmarket to improve short-term sales, the following companies produced high quality pens that are collected in most world markets, and they rarely sell for more than $1,500.

Carter	Kosca	Edward Todd
Caw	Partner	Wahl-Eversharp
Chilton	Pelikan	Well
A. T. Cross	Schnell	Paul E. Wirt
Heath	Sheaffer	

ABOVE **A 1927 advertisement for Wahl-Eversharp.**

ABOVE **1920s lever-filler by Wahl-Eversharp; 6¼ inches. Sterling silver was used for the** "brains pattern" vermeil **decoration. Of the numerous models of metal pens produced in the late 1920s by Wahl, the two-tone vermeil pattern is the most sought after.**

ABOVE **1899 Paul E. Wirt gold-filled twist pattern; 4¾ inches.**

HIGH-VALUE PENS NOT WIDELY DISTRIBUTED

Top quality pens by the following companies can be worth as much as examples from the first category, but the names are relatively unknown outside the home markets, and the pens, therefore, tend not to be as widely collected. Again, the difficulties of obtaining good quality materials during war-time should be borne in mind.

FRANCE

Météore	Laureau

GERMANY

Astoria	Osmia	Soennecken
Goldfink	Reform	

ITALY

Ancora	Everest	Tabo
Anglo-American	Montegrappa	Williamson
Columbus	Nettuno	(of Turin)

JAPAN

Platinum	Sailor

UNITED KINGDOM

Ford	Phillips (generally Swan pens, distributed by a shop called Phillips in Oxford)

UNITED STATES

Aikin Lambert	Hicks	J. G. Rider
Betzler & Wilson	John Holland	Sager
Camel	Houston Pen Company	Sanford & Bennett
Carey	Lancaster	Sterling
Edison	Laughlin	Triad
Eisenstadt	Lipic	Webster
Grieshaber	Monroe	Weidlich

RIGHT **1927 Grieshaber. This baby pen was made by the Chicago company during the 1920s when, for a short time, it was fashionable to enamel over hard rubber or, sometimes, silver.**

LEFT **Aikin Lambert gold-filled, high relief floral pattern eyedropper; 5¼ inches.**

BELOW **1902 Swan gold-plated diamond-cut eyedropper; 5¼ inches. Most manufacturers made pens in a diamond-cut design, but each had their own version.**

QUALITY PENS OF LESSER VALUE

The following companies did not produce top quality
pens, or they produced pens of medium size or quality,
or they were in production at a time when it was
difficult to obtain good quality materials. Alternatively,
they produced few, if any, outstanding models, or their
models were indistinguishable from those of other
companies. Their pens can form the basis of a
collection and in general, they can write well.

CANADA

Eclipse

FRANCE

Bayard	Jif-Waterman	Le Mallet Tigré
Edacoto	*(unless in metal)*	*(but very valuable if*
Gold Starry	Stylomine	*pre-1880s)*

GERMANY

Geha	Matador	*by Montblanc with*
Grief	Reform	*a warranted nib*
Johann Faber	Stædtler-Mars	*identifiable by a*
Lamy *(called Artus*	Reflex *(a better*	*triangle or diamond-*
or Orthos)*	quality student pen*	*square in the center)*

ITALY

Tibaldi

ISRAEL

Katab

UNITED KINGDOM

Blackbird	Mackinnon	Post
Conway Stewart	McNiven &	Summit
Dickinson	Cameron	Swallow
Jewel Pen	Mentmore	Valentine
Company	National Security	Wyvern

RIGHT **Early 1930s Dinky lever-filler by Conway Stewart; 3¾ inches.**

LEFT **1930s lever-filler by Conway Stewart; 4⅝ inches. This multicolored pen has an earlier style of lever and, overall, exhibits a remarkable degree of quality for this manufacturer.**

ABOVE **1930s Dinky lever-filler by Conway Stewart; 3¾ inches; box 4¼ inches.**

UNITED STATES

Century	*Pen Company*	*tiny sizes, such as*
Diamond Medal	*of Chicago or, later,*	*Peter Pan, but not*
Diamond Point	*A.A. Waterman, etc.)*	*as combination pen/*
Eagle	J. Harris	*pencils)*
Gold Bond	Postal	Williamson *(of*
Good Service Pen	Rexall	*Janesville,*
Company *(or*	Salz *(low quality pens*	*Wisconsin)*
Lincoln or National	*still collectable in*	Wilrite

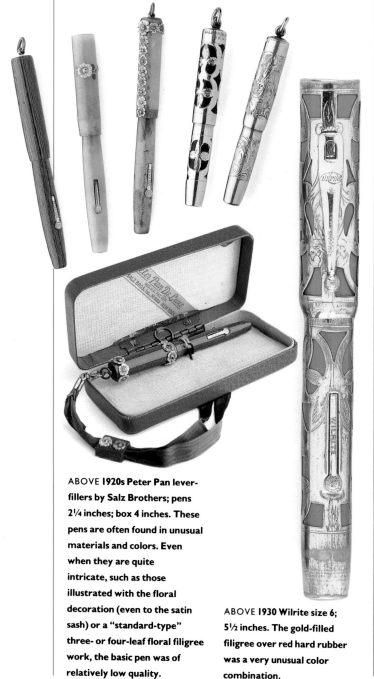

ABOVE 1920s Peter Pan lever-fillers by Salz Brothers; pens 2¼ inches; box 4 inches. These pens are often found in unusual materials and colors. Even when they are quite intricate, such as those illustrated with the floral decoration (even to the satin sash) or a "standard-type" three- or four-leaf floral filigree work, the basic pen was of relatively low quality.

ABOVE 1930 Wilrite size 6; 5½ inches. The gold-filled filigree over red hard rubber was a very unusual color combination.

LOW-VALUE PENS

In general, these pens were poorly made from second-rate materials and often in only small sizes. They usually had gold-plated, glass or plastic nibs, although occasionally they are found with warranted nibs. Because of their construction they have not survived the 40 or so years since their manufacture in good condition. They will not form the basis of a collection unless price is the determining factor. Alternatively, they were relatively poorly made by the major manufacturers (whose names are indicated in brackets) to be sold cheaply to the student market.

GOLD-NIBBED PENS

All American	Merlin	*Esterbrook and*
(made by Conklin)	Morrison *(but*	*used in very cheap*
Boots	*check all gold*	*pens)*
Burnham	*markings carefully*	Seal
Croxley	*for veracity)*	Stephens
Epenco *(made by*	Parkette *(made by*	Tropen
Eagle)	*Parker)*	Unique
A. W. Faber	Relief *(a high quality*	Wasp *(made by*
Hudson	*nib made by the*	*Sheaffer)*
Kritzler	*company for*	

GLASS-POINTED NIB PENS

Melbi

Spohr

ABOVE **Glass (plastic) nib.**

TIN OR GOLD-PLATED NIB PENS

Ambassador	Ingersoll	Paramount
Atoya	Jackdaw *(made by*	Platignum
Autofiller	*Mabie, Todd and*	*(made by*
Banker	*often having a base*	*Mentmore)*
Conklin	*metal nib)*	Rötring
(post-1940)	Leeds	Stratford
Esterbrook	New Clip	Uhü
Faber-Castell	Osmiroid *(made by*	Waterson
Foreign	*Perry)*	Wearever

USEFUL ADDRESSES

FOUNTAIN PEN CLUBS

BELGIUM
Belgian Pen Collectors Association
Postbus 71, 1000 Brussels
Publications: De Ganzepen/La Plume
D'Ole (quarterly)

ITALY
Italian Academy of Fountain Pens
Viale Del Garibaldini 64,
58035 Braccagni (Grosseto)
Publications: Stylomania (Quarterly,
bilingual English/Italian)
Holds annual pen show in Florence or
Grosseto

International Club of Fountain Pens
(A. Simoni)
Via del Fonditore 10, 40138 Bologna
Publications: Club Internazionale Della
Penna Stilografica (quarterly, bilingual
English/Italian)
Holds biannual shows in Milan and is
planning pen shows in Rome, Madrid,
Tokyo.

USA
Pen Collectors of America
P.O. Box 821449
Houston, Texas
Publications: The Pennant (quarterly)

GENERAL DIPPING PEN/ PENCIL CLUBS

FRANCE
The Pen Collectors' Club
7, Rue Des Epinettes, 75015 Paris
Publication: Au Fil De La Plume
(quarterly)

GERMANY
International Forum of Historical Office
Environments
Im Grund 58 Dw-4W D-4000
Dusseldorf 30
Publication: HBw Aktuell (quarterly)

UK
Writing Equipment Society
4 Greystones Grange Crescent, Sheffield
S11 7JL
Publication: Journal of the WES
(quarterly)

MUSEUM

FRANCE
Armando Simoni International Pen
Museum
Centre Culturel des Capuchins
7 Rue Lambin
Montfort L'Amaury
Nr. Paris

> If any reader wishes to contact the author for advice on acquisition or disposal of any fountain pen, please feel free to do so through the publishers.

INDEX

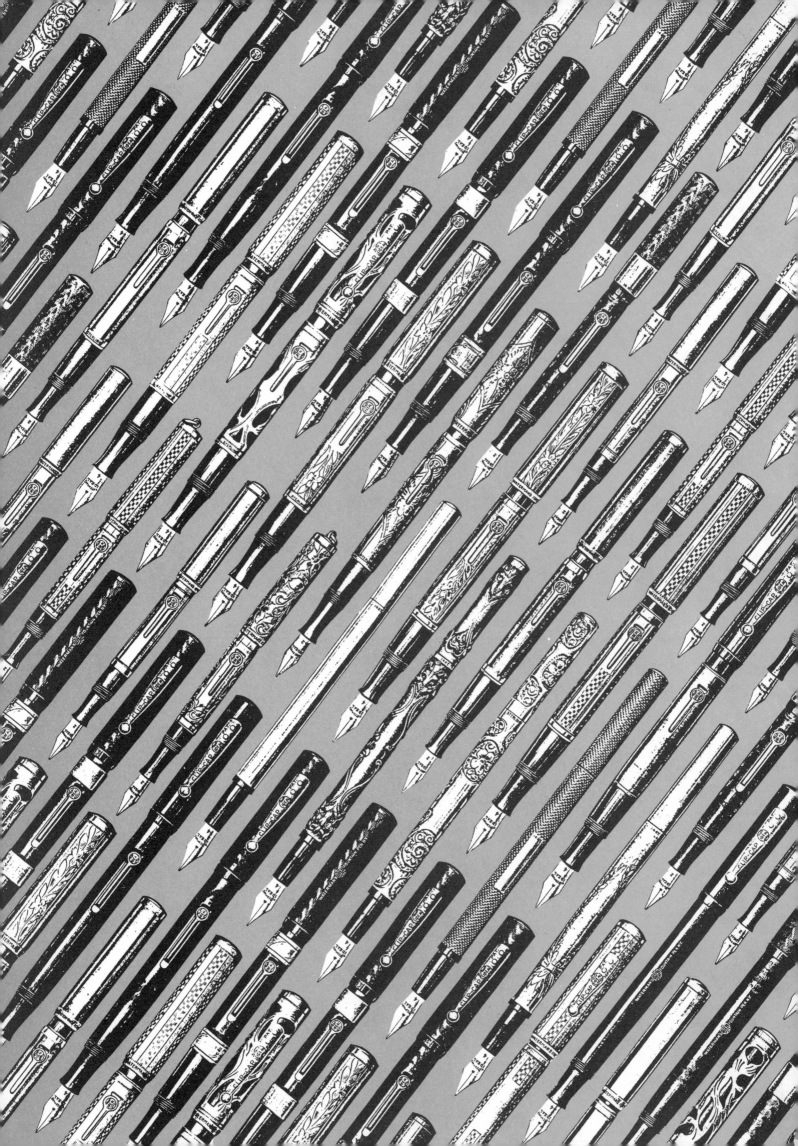